JOAN OF ARC
WARRIOR SAINT

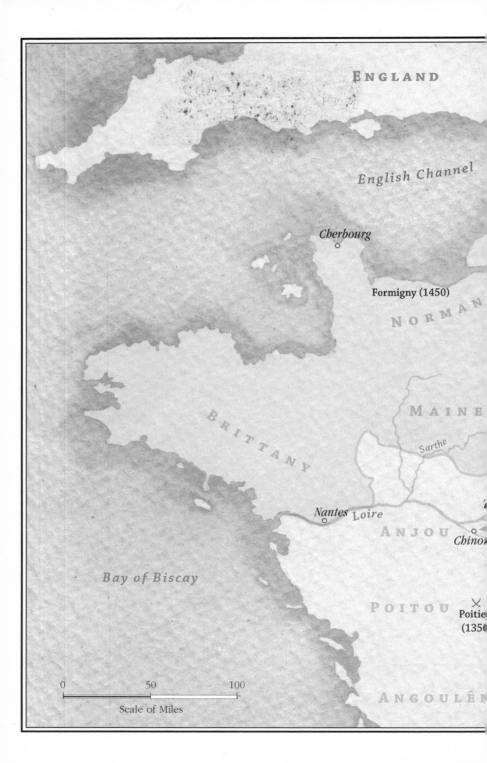

Calais

FLANDERS

BRABANT

ARTOIS

✗ Agincourt (1415)

✗ Crécy (1346)   Arras

PICARDY

Joan of Arc's
FRANCE
1429

Territory Controlled by
England & Burgundy

Meuse

Oise

Beauvais   Choisy   Soissons
Margny
Compiègne

ouen

Reims

Marne

CHAMPAGNE

Châlons

St. Denis

Lagny

Paris Vincennes

Moselle

LORRAINE

Vaucouleurs

Domrémy

hartres

Melun

Bray

Seine

Aube

Janville

audun

atay ✗ Orleans

Yeung ✗

Beaugency

Blois

Jargeaux

Sully

Troyes

Yonne

Auxerre

Cher

Bourges

INE

Dijon

BURGUNDY

enonceaux

Indre

Loire

BERRY

Allier

BOURBON

Lake Geneva

Creuse

RCHE

Lyon

Joan of Arc statue in Quebec City, Canada

JOAN OF ARC
WARRIOR SAINT

JAY WILLIAMS

STERLING

New York / London
www.sterlingpublishing.com/kids

A FLYING POINT PRESS BOOK

Design: PlutoMedia and John T. Perry III
Front cover painting: Allen Douglas
Frontispiece: Benôit Jolivet

STERLING and the distinctive Sterling logo are registered trademarks of
Sterling Publishing Co., Inc.

Library of Congress Cataloging in Publication Data

Williams, Jay, 1914–1978.
Joan of Arc : warrior saint / Jay Williams.
p. cm. — (Sterling point books)
Includes index.
ISBN-13: 978-1-4027-5120-2
ISBN-10: 1-4027-5120-6

1. Joan, of Arc, Saint, 1412–1431—Juvenile literature. 2. France—History—Charles VII, 1422–1461—
Juvenile literature. 3. Christian saints—France—Biography—Juvenile literature. 4. France—History—
Charles VII, 1422–1461—Juvenile literature. I. Title. II. Title: Warrior saint. III. Title: Sterling Point
books Joan of Arc.

DC103.5.W5 2007
944'.026092—dc22   2007009896
[B]

2   4   6   8   10   9   7   5   3   1

Published by Sterling Publishing Co., Inc.
387 Park Avenue South, New York, NY 10016
Original edition published by American Heritage Publishing Co., Inc.
under the title *Joan of Arc*
Copyright © 1963 by American Heritage Publishing Co., Inc.
New material in this updated edition
Copyright © 2007 by Flying Point Press
Maps copyright © by Richard Thompson, Creative Freelancers, Inc.
Drawing of armor: Leroux: P.U.F.
Distributed in Canada by Sterling Publishing
c/o Canadian Manda Group, 165 Dufferin Street
Toronto, Ontario, Canada M6K 3H6
Distributed in the United Kingdom by GMC Distribution Services
Castle Place, 166 High Street, Lewes, East Sussex, England BN7 IXU
Distributed in Australia by Capricorn Link (Australia) Pty. Ltd.
P.O. Box 704, Windsor, NSW 2756, Australia

Sterling ISBN-13: 978-1-4027-5120-2
ISBN-10: 1-4027-5120-6

For information about custom editions, special sales, premium and corporate purchases, please contact
Sterling Special Sales Department at 800-805-5489 or specialsales@sterlingpub.com.

CONTENTS

CONTENTS

TODAY WHEN WE THINK OF THE GREAT CITY OF Paris, we think of inspiring monuments, fine museums, culture, learning, and fashion. Paris is now called the "City of Light." But in the fifteenth century Paris was a city of darkness. Rats and wolves roamed the streets. Plagues, poverty, and death were constant companions of the city's residents. And Paris was in the hands of the English.

England and France had been at war for a hundred years. At the time of Joan of Arc's birth, forces from England occupied half of France. The English believed that France should be a possession of England. The seeds of this dispute started when William the Conqueror invaded England in the year 1066. William was from Normandy in France. After defeating the English in the Battle of Hastings, William became King of England and England was considered a part of the Kingdom of France.

Over the next several centuries, as England became more powerful, the English kings felt that they had a claim on parts of France instead of the other way around! As a result, war broke out between the two countries. It is important to note that during this time, the idea of nations and countries was only just starting to come into being. In feudal Europe, towns, cities, and villages were under the control of a lord who usually owed allegiance to a king or prince. Those allegiances could and did change often depending on battles, treaties, and marriages.

To complicate matters, when Joan was a young girl France had no real king and leader. There was at the time a prophecy that said, "France will be lost by a woman and will be saved by a maiden." In fact, when the French King, Charles VI, died, his wife, Queen Isabelle, arranged for her daughter, Catherine, to marry the English King, Henry V. By doing this, she tried to hand over all of France, not to her son, Charles VII, but to England. Thus she was the woman who "lost" France.

Because of this, France was in grave danger of falling completely into the hands of England. Not only were the English better organized, they were also much better armed than the French. They had developed the longbow, a powerful weapon that could send long arrows into enemy lines with great force. The English used this weapon to defeat the French in battle at Agincourt in 1415. From then on, French soldiers were terrified of the well-equipped armies of England.

The world of kings, queens, and royalty was far away from the simple world into which Joan was born in 1412. Most people lived their whole lives within a mile or two of their birthplace in small villages. Work was hard and unending. Survival was a constant struggle. Formal education was almost unknown and most people were full of superstitions. They believed in magic, witches, prophecies and visions.

God and religion were a big part of people's lives at this time. The church or cathedral was the most important building in any village or city. When people were not working, they worshiped in those churches. It was important to be seen as a devout believer rather than a heretic. There was no middle ground. Priests, bishops, and other religious leaders were looked to for leadership as much as kings, dukes and counts.

In addition to threats from fighting armies, people were also in constant danger from bandits and lawless gangs who roamed the countryside. Governments were much less organized than they are today and could offer villagers little protection from outlaws.

It was into this world of danger and darkness that Joan of Arc was born and would take her place in legend as the "maiden who saved France."

THE EDITORS

CAST OF CHARACTERS

Alençon, Duke of—One of Joan's staunchest supporters and dearest friends, he was related to the Dauphin.

Baretta, Bartolomeo—An Italian knight who fought with Joan's army.

Baudricourt, Robert de—Captain of the fortress of Vaucouleurs. Joan made her first journey to appeal to him.

Bedford, Duke of—Regent of France in 1423. He held power in France for the English.

Cauchon, Pierre, Bishop of Beauvais—He was the chief judge in Joan's trial.

Charles VII—The rightful heir to the Kingdom of France. He was called the Dauphin, which is a term the French use for someone who is next in line to be king. He was excluded from royal succession by his mother, Queen Isabelle.

d'Arras, Franquet—A Burgundian captain executed by the French.

d'Aulon, Jean—Joan's squire. A squire is a young man of noble birth who is a personal attendant to a knight.

Dunois, Count of—A brave and chivalrous knight who was one of Joan's strongest supporters.

CAST OF CHARACTERS

Fastolf, Sir John—Commander of the English armies in France.

Flavy, Guillaume de—A French knight who fought for Joan's army.

Gamache, Jean de—A French knight. At first he refused to take orders from Joan but he later became a close ally.

Glasdale, William—An English captain.

Gressart, Perrinet—A Burgundian captain in charge of the town of La Charité-sur-Loire.

Henry V—King of England when Joan was born. His forces defeated the French at Agincourt in 1415.

Henry VI—King of England when Joan was captured. He was only a child of nine at the time.

La Hire—"The Angry One," he was a fierce and loyal fighter for Joan.

Lassois, Durand—Joan's older cousin who helped her on her first journey.

La Tremoïlle—The Dauphin's evil chief minister.

Luxembourg, Jean de—Duke Philip's second-in-command of the Burgundian forces.

Philip—Duke of Burgundy and an ally of the English.

Regnault—Chancellor of France and Archbishop of Chartres. He was a religious leader in France.

Talbot, Lord—The English commander of the siege of Orléans.

Suffolk, Earl of—Head of the English forces that held the city of Jargeau.

CHAPTER I

THE MAID OF LORRAINE

THE VILLAGE OF DOMRÉMY LAY IN THE PEACEFUL valley of the river Meuse. Willows and poplars grew along the river's bank, and not far from the village stretched the dark, ancient forest called the Wood of the Oaks, in which wolves and bears were known to prowl.

At the beginning of the fifteenth century, Domrémy was made up of only forty or fifty houses. Although the village was small, its loyalties were divided. One part of it was in the French duchy of Lorraine. The other part belonged to the smaller duchy of Bar, whose ruler owed allegiance not to the French crown but to an enemy alliance that threatened to overcome all of France.

One of the houses in the village just inside the border of Lorraine belonged to an ambitious farmer named Jacques d'Arc. The d'Arc house had a slate roof supported by thick beams, and a floor that was simply pounded earth. There were five children in the household, and one of them was a girl named Joan, who was born around the year 1412.

The people of Domrémy were mostly farmers, and farm life in the Middle Ages could be exceedingly grim. The peasants had to produce every necessity of life themselves: food, clothing, housing, and tools. In the manuscript pictures of the period, a woman was rarely shown without her distaff, a short staff with a mass of wool tied to the end. She carried the distaff under her arm and with busy fingers pulled and twisted the wool into yarn. The distaff was the symbol of woman's unending labor, for everyone worked—children as well as women.

As a child, Joan was often sent out to drive her father's sheep to pasture. She did not enjoy being a shepherdess, she reported later. She much preferred helping her mother with the spinning and the household chores. But even indoor work was strenuous, and Joan developed the peasant woman's stout muscles and roughened skin. She was a bright child, but like the other children who were neighbors and playmates, she could not read or write. Nor did she know her age precisely. All she knew was the farm and the village, and the church that stood near her home.

It was a life of strict routine, for the round of the year's activities seldom varied. First there was the plowing and sowing, then the harvest. And there were the ceaseless tasks of weaving, baking, tanning leather, mending tools, gardening, preserving, and gathering acorns to feed the swine. The work was interrupted only by festivals and holidays, some of which were Church feasts, others pagan in origin. Sometimes both elements were combined in a strange way, as on the fourth Sunday in Lent, called Laetare Sunday. After mass had been said in the church, the young people of the village skipped or ran off to a huge old beech tree at the edge of the forest. They sat by a stream that flowed nearby and ate winter apples, nuts, and special flat cakes baked for the occasion. Then they sang and danced to the music of country pipes and gathered wild flowers to make garlands which they hung on the beech tree.

The old tree was called the Fairies' Tree, for people said that fairies had once been seen there. The ritual in the woods had become a part of the merrymaking of feast days by the time Joan was born. The young people sang and danced because that was the local tradition—not because they still honored the ancient superstitions or actively believed in fairies.

Joan went with the others to the Fairies' Tree and to a spring called the Blackthorn Fountain that supposedly had magic powers. She hung garlands on the beech tree and joined her friends in dancing around it. These actions were later used as evidence against her, for that part of France had once been a notorious haven for witches—at least that is what people thought.

God was very real and very close to fifteenth-century man, and the Devil was a constant and fearful threat. The world was believed to be a battleground for the forces of good and evil, a setting for the constant tug of war between piety and heresy, the religious and the pagan. Only extremes could be considered in such a conflict: a man was either a believer or a heretic—if he deviated at all in his actions or beliefs, he was suspect. Perhaps he was under the spell of witchcraft; and witches had to be disposed of; burning was the usual method.

Prophecies were particularly important in that age of visions and heavenly visitations. Many of the prophecies given the most attention were those attributed to Merlin, the great magician of the King Arthur romances, who was supposed to have lived in the fifth century. The French adapted his prophecies and made them part of their lore. As interpreted by the French, one of these sayings was that their country would be ruined by a woman and saved by a maiden. This maiden, it was said, would be dressed in a man's clothes and would come from an oak forest in Lorraine. These beliefs were prevalent long before Joan was born, but soon they would be remembered and whispered again all over France.

Joan was very much like the children of Domrémy with whom she grew up; however, there were differences. The chroniclers of her life reported that birds would come down and eat from her hands and that often instead of hanging garlands on the Fairies' Tree, she would take flowers to church and offer them before the image of Saint Margaret. She was more devout than the children she played with and with whom she shared many of her secrets. And she was so eager for confession—although she was hardly old enough to have sins to confess—that the village priest would sometimes pretend to scold her. Then one sunny afternoon, everything changed for her.

She was twelve then; at least she thought so. She was in the garden of her parents' house, she recalled later, when all at once there was a great glare of light. It was on her right, from the direction of the church. And a voice coming out of the air said to her, "Be a good girl, Joan, and pious. Great things are expected of you." It was an eerie experience, and she was frightened—although the voice that spoke was gentle and reassuring. A few days later she heard it again, accompanied by the same brilliant light. When she heard it the third time, she realized who was speaking to her: the Archangel Michael, captain of the armies of heaven and defender of France.

He was winged and glorious, she said later, and surrounded by a multitude of glittering angels. One of her chroniclers wrote that Joan said she recognized Saint Michael "by the angels' speech and tongue," that at first she had doubts, but then the Archangel "taught her and showed her so many things that she firmly believed it was he."

The vision came often—sometimes three times a week, she recalled—and then one day the voice announced to her, "Saint Catherine and Saint Margaret will visit you in my place, for they have been appointed to guide and counsel you. Believe what they say to you, and do as they direct, for such is the will of God."

Joan was especially devoted to these two saints and often had offered prayers to them. Both were said to have been virgins who died for their faith. They appeared to her finally as queens with golden crowns on their heads and a perfumelike fragrance about them. They called Joan Daughter of God, and she fell on her knees and embraced their feet in humility and piety. To them she vowed to remain a virgin all her life.

No one knows if Joan told anybody of her visitations at the time. Her priest may have heard about them, but the seal of the confessional would have kept him silent anyway. She said later that she heard the voices best in the rustle of leaves and in the ringing of church bells.

For more than four years the voices counseled her, telling her to be good and live a pure and pious life. Then one day Saint Michael came to her with a new command, one that Saint Catherine and Saint Margaret continued to repeat.

"Daughter of God," he said, "you must leave your native village and go to aid your king." When she heard these words, Joan began to weep. She wept out of fear, for what could she, a poor country girl, do to help her ruler? And she wept out of pity. There was good reason for pity; the kingdom of France was in grave danger of collapse.

For nearly a hundred years France had been at war with England over the right to the French crown. At Crécy and Poitiers, two great battles of this so-called Hundred Years' War, English forces had swept away French armies two and three times their number. And in scores of smaller engagements the English had given France the habit of defeat. French soldiers learned to fear more than anything the terrible English longbow; it killed their horses as they galloped into battle, and with deadly accuracy could punch a thirty-inch arrow into the eye slit of a helmet from a hundred yards away.

In 1415 King Henry V of England defeated the French decisively at Agincourt. A few years later a treaty was drawn up between the two countries at Troyes. By the terms of the agreement, Henry was declared heir to the throne of France and given the hand of Catherine, daughter of France's mad King Charles VI.

This treaty was the political and historical reason for

France's division into two parts. But by 1423 the kings who had initiated the treaty were dead, and now the reason for the split had more to do with might than with right.

English might was wielded by John, Duke of Bedford, who acted as regent of France for the infant king, Henry VI. Bedford had no easy task before him. He decided that his mission of bringing France completely under England's control might be carried out more easily by strengthening the alliance that had been made with the Duke of Burgundy. For that Duke, who did not recognize the sovereignty of the French ruler, was all too willing to send his rough soldiery out to ravage the French countryside. By 1427 most of the north and east portions of France were under the domination of England and Burgundy, the Anglo-Burgundian alliance; only parts of the west and south remained loyal to the crown.

But there was no French crown—that is, no one actually wore it. Charles VII, the rightful but disinherited heir to France, was not yet king. His mother, Queen Isabelle, had hinted he was illegitimate, and the Treaty of Troyes had excluded him from the royal succession. In the eyes of the common people he was the Dauphin—that is, the Prince of Dauphiné (just as the heir to the British crown is called the Prince of Wales). He was surrounded by councilors who cared only for their own gain, and by factions that bickered constantly among themselves. His chief minister was the fat and evil La Tremoïlle, whose main interest was collecting money and personal power. La Tremoïlle had murdered his first wife for her wealth and had then assassinated his chief rival at court for a position next to the throne. He loaned money to those he wanted to have in his debt—including the impoverished Dauphin—and used his position to carry on private wars against his enemies.

So France was divided between the English and Burgundians on one side and the French Dauphin on the other. And the land itself was rent by both friends and enemies. All over the countryside bands of ruffians roamed. Some were groups of Spaniards, Italians, or Scots who had been brought in as mercenaries of the French but had turned to thievery. Others were local knights who took what they could. Every town had a sentry in a tower, and at the sound of his bell or horn, even the sheep and pigs would run for shelter.

Jacques d'Arc, Joan's father, had taken precautions to protect the people of Domrémy. He and one of his neighbors had succeeded in renting an unused castle on a small island in the Meuse. This castle became a refuge for the villagers whenever marauding bands threatened them. Many times during Joan's childhood, a sentry's alarm in the dead of night sent her and her family tumbling out of their beds, hastening to the tiny castle with what few belongings they could carry clutched to their chests. France had become a lawless country; her people were vulnerable to enemies both from without and within.

In 1428 England set the stage for what was expected to be France's final collapse and sent a new army across the Channel to wipe out what was left of the resistance. By this time, many of France's once-loyal barons had deserted the cause; hope and prayer were all that were left to Charles VII. "He was without support," said a chronicler; "he lacked advice, he was penniless and soldierless, yet his heart was filled with love for his realm."

CHAPTER 2

JOAN LEAVES HOME

JOAN'S VOICES HAD BEEN SAYING OVER AND OVER, "Daughter of God, why do you wait? Great is the need. Leave your village and go to France."

She had replied, often with tears, "I am a poor girl. I do not know how to make war."

"Take the standard sent by the King of Heaven," her voices told her. "Take it boldly and God will help you."

Then at last Saint Michael spoke again, and his instructions were more specific: "Daughter of God, go to Robert de Baudricourt, who is captain of the fortress of Vaucouleurs. He will give you men-at-arms to take you to the Dauphin." It was her duty, the Archangel said, to relieve the siege of Orléans, to lead the Dauphin to Reims where he would be crowned, and to drive the English at last from France.

Joan was stunned, but Saint Michael told her not to be frightened. Saint Catherine and Saint Margaret would guide her on her way; her journey to Vaucouleurs would be made without harm or hindrance.

She did not inform her parents of the Archangel's commands, for she knew they would forbid her to obey them. Coincidentally Joan's father had been troubled by a dream in which he saw his daughter going off with some soldiers. This offended his moral sense, for in the Middle Ages respectable girls went away from home only to marry or join a convent, not to accompany soldiers. The dream upset Jacques d'Arc so much that he told his sons, "If I really believed this would happen, I should want you to drown her, and if you would not, I would drown her with my own hands."

Joan was resolved to do as her voices had commanded, but she knew she also needed assistance of a more earthly nature than her saints could offer. She turned to a man named Durand Lassois. He was her cousin by marriage, but because he was sixteen years her senior she called him uncle. He and his wife lived in a neighboring village, and Joan was accustomed to visiting them. She went to see Lassois and told him of her visions.

"I shall defeat the English," she proclaimed boldly; for by then her confidence had soared. "And I will take the

Dauphin to Reims to be crowned king. You must escort me to Vaucouleurs to see Robert de Baudricourt."

Lassois was a patient, agreeable man, but he must have been astonished by his young cousin's request. He hesitated, but Joan reminded him of the prophecy "France was lost by a woman and will be saved by a maiden." The first part of the prophecy had already come to pass. The malevolent Queen Isabelle, allied with the Duke of Burgundy, had been instrumental in bringing about the Treaty of Troyes, which had ceded France to the English kings.

Lassois must also have remembered that according to the prophecy the virgin who was to save France would come from an oak forest—and that such a forest lay near Joan's birthplace at Domrémy. However, Joan's conviction, her absolute certainty that God Himself was directing her actions, must have carried more weight. Or perhaps his terror of the advancing English was such that he felt compelled to pursue any opportunity that presented itself. For in the end he agreed to be Joan's guide and protector on the journey to Vaucouleurs.

Robert de Baudricourt, captain of the fortress, was in the service of Charles VII. He was a tough soldier and a good knight, and he had a merry humor. It is possible Joan had heard of him before, for her father had once visited him as a representative from Domrémy to discuss a dispute over the payment of taxes. It is also possible she knew what he looked like. Or perhaps she knew intuitively who he was. In any event, she easily found him among the crowd of men-at-arms and citizens who filled the great hall at Vaucouleurs on that day in May 1428.

She wore a patched red dress and her head was covered with a kerchief as she appeared before Sir Robert. Her hair beneath the kerchief was dark, and she had a pleasant, womanly voice. Baudricourt probably expected to hear some local complaint from the sixteen-year-old village girl, whose quiet companion stood in the background, twisting his hat between his hard fingers.

Joan spoke without hesitation: "I have been sent to you by my Lord to tell you to give this message to the Dauphin. He must not cease to resist his enemies, but he must beware of giving battle to them. Before Mid-Lent my Lord will send him help."

Baudricourt was doubtless puzzled that some nobleman who wished to help the Dauphin should have sent a peasant girl as his messenger. He asked, "Who is your Lord?"

"He is the King of Heaven," said Joan.

Baudricourt was astounded, and Joan went on: "It is my Lord's will that the Dauphin shall be king and shall hold

France as the vassal of God. I myself will lead him to be anointed and crowned."

Baudricourt regained his senses and reacted harshly, almost belligerently, to what seemed to him mere nonsense. "Take her home to her father," he directed Lassois, "and tell him to give her a good thrashing."

Joan and her escort left the fortress. Although somewhat discouraged, she was undismayed. She returned home and waited. Meanwhile France's crucial hour drew closer at hand.

The English troops sent by the Duke of Bedford to mop up the last of the French resistance were victorious everywhere they went. In October 1428, they consolidated their strength and threw all their forces into a siege of Orléans. This city was France's most important remaining stronghold. If it fell, her cause would be hopeless.

By the end of the year, Joan's voices were becoming more insistent. Finally, when she could resist them no longer, she made Lassois agree to take her back to Vaucouleurs. They set out together on a bitter morning in January 1429.

Baudricourt remembered her when she stood before him once more. And she said, "My lord captain, God has again commanded me to appear before you. You must send me to the Dauphin. He will give me soldiers and I will rescue the city of Orléans. Then I will take him to Reims to be anointed."

This time Baudricourt did not scoff at her, but neither did he agree to help her. So Joan and Lassois settled down in the fortress town of Vaucouleurs to wait for the captain to make up his mind.

News of the peasant girl who claimed to have been sent by God to save the kingdom spread throughout the district. People were reminded of the old prophecies and came to see the maid. To everyone she said, "I must go to the Dauphin even if I must wear out my legs to the knees." Two noblemen were sufficiently impressed by her to promise that they would help persuade Baudricourt to send her to the Dauphin. They were Bertrand de Poulengy and Jean de Metz, young squires in the service of the captain. But Joan grew impatient, and one day she burst suddenly into the great hall of the fortress and confronted Baudricourt. It was February 12, a date he would long remember.

"In God's name," she cried, "you have done ill to delay in sending me! This very day, near Orléans, a great disaster has taken place. Why did you not tell the Dauphin to avoid battle with the enemy as I warned him?" Baudricourt had heard of no great battle, disastrous or otherwise, and promptly dismissed her.

Not many days later the captain and a priest paid an unexpected visit to Joan in the house of the wheelwright where she was staying. The priest put on his stole and uttered words that were supposed to exorcise demons: "If you be a thing of evil, be gone from us," he said to Joan; "if you be from God, approach us."

Joan was angry, for, as she said later, the priest had heard her confess in church and should have known her to be a devout Catholic. However, she went to him and fell on her knees for a blessing, thereby indicating—at least to the priest and to Baudricourt—that she was not a witch.

Why had Baudricourt come to her? Why had he chosen this particular time to test her faith? It was learned, finally, that on the day Joan had burst in to see him, February 12, an English army of some thousand archers and twelve hundred Burgundian pikemen had been attacked near Orléans by a French force almost twelve times bigger. The English commander, Sir John Fastolf, had been taking a shipment of herring to the English troops that surrounded the walled city when the French fell upon him.

Quickly he had drawn up the wagons into a square. His archers were positioned behind the barrels of fish; the spearmen were between them. The French dashed themselves uselessly against this formation and were finally forced to withdraw. It was another humiliating French defeat, which the English referred to mockingly as the Battle of the

Herrings. They were certain now that Orléans would soon be plucked from French control and the exhausting, costly Hundred Years' War would be over.

The fact that Joan had warned against the Battle of the Herrings, and had actually known of it the very day it took place, won Robert de Baudricourt to her favor. Now the captain resolved that she should go to the Dauphin. Both Jean de Metz and Bertrand de Poulengy were among her six escorts.

On a day in late February, in the mist and chill, Joan and her companions mounted their horses. Joan had dressed herself as a man, since she was to travel with men and pass through enemy territory where she might be captured. She wore a tunic and trousers, spurred boots, and a black cap. She had cut her hair short like that of a page.

Baudricourt had given her a horse and a dagger right for her use. It was a short, lightweight weapon whose slender grip fitted easily into her small hand. He made the six men swear an oath that they would guard Joan and guide her safely to the town of Chinon, where the Dauphin then had his court.

"Go!" he said at last. "And come what may." The company trotted out through the Gate of France on the road to the west.

CHAPTER 3

THE MAID MEETS THE DAUPHIN

FROM VAUCOULEURS TO THE ROYAL CASTLE AT Chinon was about 350 miles. It would have been a substantial trip even for a soldier hardened to the rigors of travel. But for a country girl like Joan, whose only experience on horseback had been on her father's farm and whose longest journey had been less than thirty miles, it was like traveling to another continent.

To avoid contact, if possible, with their ever-present enemies, Joan and her escorts traveled mainly on back roads—which made the trip more difficult. So did the necessity of muffling the horses' hooves with cloth and of riding only at night when passing towns where hostile troops were concentrated.

Never once during the ride did Joan lose her courage, and she repeatedly assured her companions that they would suffer no harm. She remained calm and cheerful, and when Jean de Metz once asked her curiously, "Will you really do all you say?" she replied, "Have no fear. I do what I am commanded to do."

Sleeping on the ground, in stables, and more rarely at monasteries; crossing rivers in which the broken ice crunched menacingly; and riding through the cold wetness of February, the group completed the journey in about eleven days.

On March 6, 1429, Joan entered Chinon. It was Laetare Sunday, that very Sunday in Lent on which Joan and her friends had once hung garlands on the Fairies' Tree. She was far removed from the pastimes of her childhood now. Looking above the town, to the north, she could see the proud, rounded towers of one of France's finest castles. There, in dismal poverty, dwelt the uncrowned king she had come so far and waited so long to see.

Before riding into Chinon, she had stopped in the town of Fierbois to worship before the statue of Saint Catherine in the church there, and also to dictate a letter to the Dauphin. In this letter she explained that she had "many excellent revelations" for the Dauphin, and that to prove her claims she would recognize him among any number of people.

Soon after her arrival, Joan was visited by a deputation of

clergymen who had come to question her on behalf of Charles VII. All that she would tell them was that she had come with two commands from the King of Heaven: to relieve the siege of Orléans and to take Charles VII to Reims to be anointed and crowned. The next day she was summoned into the royal presence.

The audience chamber of the castle was lighted by scores of torches burning in iron brackets on the walls. Their dancing yellow light glimmered on the golden chains, the furs, the polished swords, and the trailing gowns of over three hundred noblemen and ladies. In this splendid gathering Joan stood out more sharply than if she had been dressed in cloth of gold. She was still wearing the costume in which she had traveled, and even if she felt out of place she appeared unembarrassed, standing straight-backed and quiet, her face aglow with the sense of her divine mission.

Legend has it that someone gestured toward the richly dressed Count of Clermont, indicating to Joan that he was the Dauphin. But Joan is alleged to have replied, "That is not he. I shall recognize him when I see him."

Charles VII, who was twenty-six at this time, was not a distinguished-looking man. He was not tall, and his thin legs looked almost too weak to support him. A later portrait of him by the painter Jean Fouquet shows a face both melancholy and sensitive, but rather ugly, with full, pouting lips, a large nose whose tip was bulbous, and small, heavy-lidded eyes. His ill-fitting clothes hung on him, and it was known that for economy's sake he often had new sleeves sewn on to prolong the life of his old tunics.

As Joan entered the chamber Charles was standing with a group of courtiers near the immense fireplace in which a whole tree trunk was burning. Joan went up to him without hesitation, took off her cap, and bowed deeply. "God send you long life, gentle Dauphin," she said in her sweet voice, and the murmuring crowd was reduced to a hush.

Joan said later that her voices had revealed the Dauphin's identity to her, although many historians are convinced that one of Joan's companions pointed him out to her. Another school of thought suggests that if a girl as bright and intuitive as Joan had known anything at all about Charles VII and his miserable, impoverished life, she would have had no trouble picking him out of a crowd, voices or no. At any rate, the Dauphin asked her to identify herself and explain why she had come.

"I am called Joan the Maid," she answered. "I have been sent by God to take you to Reims to be anointed. Give me soldiers and I will raise the siege of Orléans, for it is God's will that the English shall leave France and return to their own country."

The Dauphin then said, "What proof have you to show that

you will do as you say?" Joan replied that she would offer him proof, but only in secret. So Charles drew her aside, motioning for the courtiers to clear a wide space around him. He and Joan talked earnestly together, although no one could hear what was said. It was observed, however, that his face lighted up with a rare smile of joy.

The matter of what Joan actually said to the Dauphin has never been settled. A story that has survived the centuries is that she told Charles she knew of a secret prayer he had once made, a prayer that God give him help to drive out the English if he were the true heir to the crown. Joan reportedly said to him with absolute conviction: "My lord, I can tell you that you are indeed the true son and heir of your father, the late king, and it is God's will that I shall raise the siege of Orléans and that you shall be anointed and crowned in Reims."

Whatever Joan actually said to the Dauphin—and eyewitnesses insisted that she told him something that moved him deeply—the Dauphin was persuaded that Joan was what she said she was. She was lodged in one of the castle towers and given a page to attend her and a lady to serve her. But Charles' councilors were not convinced by her; nor would they ever cease resenting her influence on the Dauphin. And high officials of the Church were reluctant to accept Joan as a representative of heaven. They persuaded Charles to have the girl who called herself Joan the Maid investigated by theologians to determine whether she had really come from God or the Devil. It was decided to send her to Poitiers, where many renowned scholars from the University of Paris had taken refuge.

So a commission composed of doctors and professors of canon law and theology was established. It was headed by Regnault of Chartres, Chancellor of France and Archbishop of Reims. Joan was brought before the commission and subjected to a strict cross-examination. One professor of theology hurled this challenge at her: "According to you, your voices say that God wishes to deliver the people of France from their distress. But if He wishes to deliver them, there is no need of soldiers."

Joan replied, "In God's name, the soldiers will fight and God will give the victory."

A rather sour-faced monk asked her what language her voices spoke. "A better one than yours," she answered, and everyone laughed, for the monk was from Limousin, a province farther south, and spoke a regional dialect.

The men questioned her further, and finally she said, "I do not know A from B, but God has sent me to raise the siege of Orléans . . ." They said something about the necessity of examining her according to their books of law, and she answered, "My Lord has a book in which there is more than in all of yours." They asked her for a sign; not the private sign she had given to Charles, but a public sign to prove that she had come from God. She said sharply, "In God's name, I have not come to Poitiers to give a sign. But take me to Orléans and I will show you the signs for which I am sent."

The scholars could not help being impressed. Joan's honesty and fearlessness—and her absolute certainty of the mission she had to perform—won them over. To the royal council they reported, "There has been found no evil in her, nothing but good, humility . . . devoutness, honesty, simplicity . . ." And bowing to her urgent request to go to Orléans, they recommended that she be sent there "in due state trusting to God."

CHAPTER 4

JOAN'S FIRST MISSION

SO IT WAS DECIDED, AND PREPARATIONS WERE made at once for an army to be assembled. Joan was given her own bodyguard and attendants, including a personal squire and a chaplain.

The most valuable gift Charles VII gave the Maid was a suit of armor that was made to her measurements before she rode off to Orléans. Buckled into it, Joan looked like a smaller version of the typical fifteenth-century knight: she wore the helmet, the cuirass (or body covering), the various leg pieces, and the six separate parts for each arm. Joan's steel cap was properly called a salade; but unlike most, hers was not fitted with a visor or a chin protector. In some battles she may have worn a basinet, a type of helmet with a hinged and ventilated visor. She wanted her face to show clearly, for her purpose was not to fight, but to lead by being seen—and heard.

Her cuirass, or body armor, was flexible and was made up of many parts which were held together by straps. Wherever plate armor could not be provided, chain armor filled the gaps. The total weight of all this defensive equipment—including the shoulder and elbow guards, the greaves (or shin guards), and the heavy gauntlets—was about fifty pounds. The maid's armor was "white." That is, it was bereft of crests or decorations—simple and plain as befitted one who was not a knight.

Joan's standard (or flag) bore the image of Christ seated upon a rainbow; in one hand he held the world, and the other was raised in blessing. Two kneeling angels presented to Him the fleurs-de-lis, the lilies of France. In the background were scattered the royal lilies, and written in gold letters was Joan's motto, *Jhesus-Maria.*

To complete her military equipment, the Dauphin offered her a fine sword, but she refused it. Instead, she said that her voices had told her of a sword that was buried in the ground behind the altar in the Church of St. Catherine at Fierbois, the little village from which she had first written to the Dauphin. The sword would be recognized by the five crosses it bore.

People were puzzled, for no one knew that such a sword existed. But so great was their faith in Joan that an armorer was sent to Fierbois with a letter from Joan asking the priests

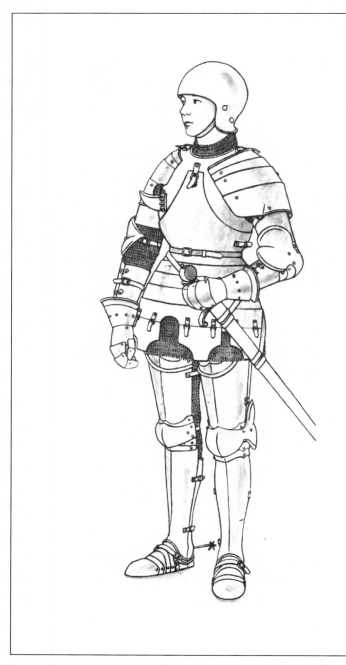

Cuirass

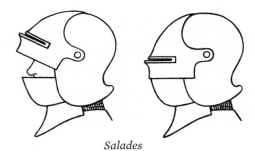

Salades

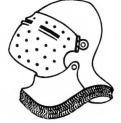

Basinets

at St. Catherine's to try to unearth the sword. The priests dutifully searched about, and in a forgotten chest buried in a niche behind the altar they found the weapon, covered with rust. As soon as the church people began to clean it, the rust flaked off without any difficulty. The five crosses were there, cut into the steel of the blade, just as Joan had predicted. It was a small miracle, but a miracle indeed, and Joan's prestige rose further as a result.

Horses were also furnished for the Maid's contingent, and a particular favorite of hers was the mount given to her by the Duke of Alençon, who was to be one of her staunchest supporters. News of Joan's arrival had brought him to Chinon, and he had arrived the day after her first meeting with the Dauphin. Alençon was related by marriage to the Dauphin and was one of the most powerful noblemen in France. His father had fallen at the Battle of Agincourt; he himself, a young man of twenty-four, had been taken prisoner by the English five years before and had only recently bought his freedom. When Joan met him, she said, "You have come at a good time. The more of the royal blood there are together, the better."

The next day they walked out to a meadow where there was a post from which hung a ring. The knights used to practice riding against this post with their lances—the object being to catch the ring on their lance heads. Joan was agile, though inexperienced, and she rode so well and handled her lance so lightly that Alençon gave her a horse on the spot.

They became dear friends, and she called him "my fair Duke." Supposedly, Alençon's young duchess once told Joan she feared for her husband's life if he went to war again. But the Maid replied, "Madame, have no fear. I will bring him back to you safely, either as he is now or better."

Alençon was charged with assembling an army at Blois, a city part-way between Chinon and Orléans. And to Joan's standard flocked not only knights and squires but common men; not only men-at-arms who served for pay or feudal duty, but volunteers from towns and farms. For them the Maid had become a symbol of hope, something France had lost until then. Some of the great warriors were skeptical, however. At first they could not believe that a peasant girl could know anything about the art of war, for they themselves had learned the hard way—in tournaments, skirmishes, and battle after battle. Yet many, like Alençon, quickly fell under the spell of her personality. One of these was a powerful bear of a man whose nickname was La Hire, which meant the Angry One.

Another was a nobleman named Jean, who later became the Count of Dunois. He was called the Bastard of Orléans, for he was the illegitimate son of the murdered Duke of Orléans. In those days there was no shame in being the illegitimate son of a prince. Dunois' half-brother, the young Duke Charles of Orléans, had been captured by the English, so Dunois took over the defense of the city shortly after the siege was begun. He was a brave and chivalrous knight who, though only twenty-six, had already distinguished himself in many battles. When news of the Maid reached him, he sent two of his captains to Chinon to learn more about her, and he was later to say, "I believe that Joan was sent by God." However, his first meeting with her was blessed with few pleasantries.

Led by La Hire and other famous warriors, the army had set out from Blois on April 27, 1429. Accounts vary, so it is impossible to indicate exactly how many troops there were—between three and four thousand, no doubt. In addition, there were herds of cattle and sheep, and wagonloads of grain for the hungry citizens of Orléans. Joan's mettle was being tested—to see how successful she would be in getting provisions into the beleaguered city of Orléans. She rode with her captains at the head of the convoy, and though she was not actually in command of the troops, the Dauphin had made it clear that "nothing shall be done without reference to the Maid, no matter how many good and competent men there may be present."

Joan's plan was simple and straightforward; she wished to be taken directly to the gates of the city so she could meet the

English commander, Lord Talbot, face to face. She wanted to give him every chance of ending the siege peacefully. But her captains, certain they knew more about warfare than she, did not believe the English would surrender. Marching right to the gates of Orléans would mean going through hostile territory and then passing by several strong fortresses held by the enemy. Thus they thought it wise to cross the Loire River into the territory controlled by France and travel east along the river's south bank to the village of Chécy. There, about five miles beyond Orléans, the convoy could be floated downstream and enter Orléans through its east gate, which was the one least strongly covered by the English.

Joan had not been informed of this strategy. As she was unfamiliar with the countryside, it was not until the convoy had passed Orléans, which was visible across the river, that she realized her more direct plan had been altered. And she was furious. When Dunois crossed the river in his small boat to greet her on her way to Chécy, he got a stinging reception. "Is it you," she cried, "who advised them to bring me here by the bank of the river instead of going straight to where Talbot and the English are?" Dunois replied politely that he and others wiser than himself had decided that this was the best course to follow. And Joan said, "In God's name, the counsel of God is wiser and surer than yours. You thought you had deceived me, but you have deceived yourselves, for I am bringing you better help than ever you got from any soldier or city. It is the help of the King of Heaven . . ."

If Joan was deceived, it was because Dunois felt it would have been folly to confront the English with a show of force before delivering food and supplies to the French troops inside the city—which, after all, had been the Maid's official mission. But in deceiving Joan, he succeeded mainly in deceiving himself—just as she had said. For now a strong wind was coming from the wrong direction, and the flotilla of heavy sail-barges that had been assembled at Orléans to sail upstream and pick up the convoy could not move. They were unable to fight both a contrary wind and a contrary current.

So Joan and her troops, and all the supplies, were stranded on the wrong side of the river. The longer they stayed there, the greater the possibility that the watchful English would discover them. It began to appear that Joan's attempt to replenish Orléans would fail because of a circumstance beyond her control. But she remained determined, despite the ill wind. Wait, she advised, and all would be well. So the convoy waited; there was nothing else to do.

What happened next was both dramatic and unexpected. Dunois, in his account of the incident, reported that the wind suddenly "changed and became favorable. Sails were therefore raised, and I brought in the ships and rafts . . . From that moment I had great hopes of [Joan], greater than before, and I begged her to cross the Loire and enter the city of Orléans where they were most eager for her . . . Then Joan came with me, carrying her white standard . . . And she crossed the river with La Hire and me, and we entered the town of Orléans together."

That was on the evening of April 29. It was eight o'clock, and hundreds of people came out to greet her, bearing torches that lit up the night. The church bells rang joyously; the citizens crowded 'round her trying to kiss her stirrups or touch her standard. They were wild with joy. The arrival of the Maid had brought a new, fresh wind blowing through the city, a breath of victory.

CHAPTER 5

BREAKING THE SIEGE OF ORLÉANS

JOAN'S ARRIVAL IN ORLÉANS THREW THE CITY into a furor. Within a day, bands of armed citizens jammed the narrow streets around the house where she was staying. Their enthusiasm was tumultuous as they clamored for her to lead them out against the English. They did not doubt that she had been sent by God to fulfill the ancient prophecy and free their land.

It is customary to think of a besieged city as one that is completely and impenetrably surrounded. But enemy troops had not closed off Orléans entirely. The English occupied forts and towers that had been built at irregular intervals around the city. The Loire River separated some of these fortifications, and three miles of open countryside lay between two of the larger towers, providing an access to the city—which was the way Joan had entered.

The city had been under siege for six months, and its supply of food was nearly depleted. Manpower was not lacking, however, for there were many more men defending Orléans than there were attacking it. What the French did lack was confidence.

Yet they were not inactive. The people had done everything they could to protect their vital city. They had even taken the extreme measure of burning the suburbs that skirted Orléans to prevent the enemy from using them for shelter. But the English built their fortresses right on the ruins and used wood, stones, and earth to put up numerous smaller fortifications that were connected by long trenches. There were also armed camps overlooking the river and the main roads.

The main English camp, where the commander, Lord Talbot, had his tents, was southwest of the city in a major for-tification called St. Laurent. Les Tourelles, on the bridge over the Loire, was another important stronghold. At the outset of the siege, an English captain named William Glasdale had captured les Tourelles. All the retreating French could do to keep the English from entering the city by way of the bridge was to break down part of it, creating an impassable gap.

The French defended Orléans stubbornly, and within a few months the siege had settled into a series of sporadic exchanges of cannon fire and brief clashes between opposing men-at-arms. The situation had reached a stalemate, and the French were becoming discouraged. There seemed no way to break the siege.

Then, suddenly, the Maid came and everything changed. People had heard of her voices, her prophecies, and the report of the examiners at Poitiers. They had waited for her eagerly, and now she was here, dressed in armor, looking like an avenging angel, the sword of Saint Catherine by her side. She had entered the city, to bring desperately needed supplies, without suffering so much as a blow. The people could not help but hope that with Joan to lead them, they might somehow defeat the English.

The more cautious barons and knights were not so captivated, however. They were a proud lot, convinced that war was a game only professionals could play. One of the knights, Jean de Gamache, expressed the feelings of his brotherhood quite baldly when he stated, "Rather than take orders from a woman I will cut my banner into a squire's [pennant] and take service under another knight."

The French leaders, unlike the common folk, had no desire to rush into battle. They urged patience—until the rest of the army arrived from Blois. Joan did not wish to plunge into combat either—not until she had tried to settle matters peaceably. She sent a letter to the English, calling upon them to leave her country. Her demand was rejected with scorn, and her herald was seized and threatened with burning.

Infuriated, Joan rode out of Orléans' south gate to the bridge and from there shouted to Glasdale to surrender. In response, the English cried out jeeringly, "Shall we surrender to a woman?" Then, threatening to burn her if she was captured, they called her a sorceress. Joan replied that they were liars and returned to the city.

On May 4, as Joan was at dinner with her squire, Jean d'Aulon, Dunois came to see her. "I have heard bad news," he began gravely. He went on to say that Sir John Fastolf, that same knight who had defeated the French in the Battle of the Herrings, was coming with supplies and reinforcements for the besiegers. This was not bad news as far as Joan was concerned; she was delighted at the chance to avenge France's honor against this foe. "In the name of God, tell me the instant Fastolf arrives," she told Dunois, "for I will not let him pass unchallenged." And she added, perhaps in jest but perhaps half in earnest, "If you let him escape me, I shall have your head." She suspected that her captains did not trust her in war, and she was fearful Dunois might withhold information from her.

Dunois agreed to let her know when Fastolf arrived. But Joan was right; he had not told her everything. He knew, while he was talking with her, that French troops were assaulting St. Loup, just east of Orléans. It was hoped that this English stronghold could be taken quickly, before Fastolf arrived with reinforcements.

When Dunois left, Joan she went upstairs for a nap. Her squire lay down on a cot in her room, for he too was very tired. Then, as he was later to tell it, the Maid sprang out of bed and woke him:

When I asked her what was the matter, she replied, "In God's name, my voices have told me that I must attack the English. But I do not know if I should go against their fortresses or against Fastolf, who is bringing them supplies." I got up quickly and armed the Maid as rapidly as I could.

While I was arming her, we heard a great noise and loud cries in the city from those who shouted that the enemy was doing great harm to the French. Then I too had myself armed, and as I was doing so the Maid left the room and went out into the street . . .

She ordered a page to fetch her horse and then sent the young man upstairs for her standard. So impatient was she, sitting astride her mount, that he was forced to hand her the standard through the window. Then with d'Aulon behind her, she spurred her horse toward the Gate of Burgundy, where the noise was loudest.

The French attack on St. Loup was not going well. As Joan galloped through the gate she met some of the French running back toward the town. "Turn about!" she cried. "The fortress is ours." The men rallied around her standard and pressed after her, as straight to the walls of the fortress she rode. The French troops were so inspired by the sight of her that they renewed the attack with furious energy.

Meanwhile, word of the attack had reached Lord Talbot, who set out from his camp with reinforcements for St. Loup. He had ridden only a short distance around Orléans before he saw thick smoke rising in the east. Obviously he was too late; the French had taken St. Loup and the fortress was in flames. He turned around and led his men back to camp.

The French were exultant. St. Loup was the first English fortification they had ever captured, and they destroyed it completely. Now there was no enemy obstacle on the east side of Orléans to prevent supplies and reinforcements from being poured into the battered city. Church bells rang out in triumph as Joan and her captains rode back through the gate.

Characteristically, Joan was less elated by the great gains of the victory than saddened by the many losses it incurred. She wept for those who had been slain, friends and foes alike. And the following day, the Feast of the Ascension, she ordered that there be no fighting, and she herself wore no armor. That day she dictated another letter to the English, which said:

You men of England, who have no right in the kingdom of France, the King of Heaven sends the order through me, Joan the Maid, to return to your own country. This is the third time I write to you, and it is the last; I will write no more.

Since the English still held her herald as a prisoner, she tied the message to an arrow and had an archer shoot it into the enemy camp. "Read, here is news!" the Maid shouted. But the English only cursed her, and she returned in tears to Orléans.

The following day, May 6, the French captains staged another attack. Their troops marched through the Gate of Burgundy and headed for St. Jean-le-Blanc, the smallest and weakest of the English forts. It was located on the south bank of the Loire, and the French made a floating bridge of barges to reach it.

Seeing the troops crossing, the English simply abandoned the fortress. They took refuge farther west, near the bridge-head, in a strong fortress built on the ruins of an Augustinian monastery. It was called les Augustins.

If Joan had been with her men at this moment (she and her mounted captains were waiting to be ferried across the river) she might have prevented what happened next. Without consulting her, the commanders of the force decided that since

St. Jean-le-Blanc had been abandoned and les Augustins was too strong to be assaulted, they would lead the soldiers back to Orléans.

The English, hoping to block the retreat and possibly erase the French contingent, swarmed out of les Augustins like angry hornets. Talbot's longbowmen planted themselves in line and loosed flight after flight of arrows on their attackers. The French were thrown into a panic. They were terrified of being surrounded by the English and caught in a deadly cross fire. It might have been a wholesale retreat had not Joan and La Hire ridden onto the scene.

Immediately Joan sent some men to guard the barges so the French could withdraw to Orléans if they had to. But this only encouraged the English to press their attack, and they did so while shouting insults at her. She had a warrior's strength and courage, but she could not bear the insults. She led her horse to the boats, intending to be ferried back to the city.

Then she had a change of heart. "In the Lord's name," she called out, "let us charge these English!" She and La Hire rode against the enemy, and the militiamen followed. The sight of the Maid, her standard raised, charging into battle, stirred them to action once again. And the English were halted. When Dunois and the other captains brought up their troops and artillery, the English took flight, retreating for shelter inside les Augustins. The French pressed the assault to the walls of the fortress and hurled volleys of cannon fire against the stronghold.

When the guns had smashed a breech in the wall, Joan called out to her troops, "Enter boldly!" The French swept in and took the stronghold. Soon it was on fire.

The barons were as pleased as Joan at the outcome of the fight, but they were slow to pick up the offensive. They chose a cautious course once again—and decided to withdraw to Orléans. The city had enough provisions now and was safe enough, they thought, to hold out until more troops arrived from the Dauphin. One of the commanders came to Joan with this message: "Glasdale and eight hundred men still hold les Tourelles at the bridgehead. Therefore the council sees no point in making a further attack tomorrow."

"While you have been at your council I have been at mine," Joan retorted. "The counsel of my Lord is better than yours." She convinced the barons that les Tourelles could be taken, and that very evening the assault on the fortress was organized.

"Rise at first light tomorrow," she ordered her chaplain. "And above all," she added, "keep close beside me, for I shall have much to do, more than at any time till now. Blood will flow from my body above my breast."

CHAPTER 6

AN ARROW FINDS JOAN

JOAN SLEPT FITFULLY THAT NIGHT; NOISES ISSUING from the English lines continually disturbed her. She was awakened at dawn, and she heard mass and had her squire arm her. As he was buckling on the steel plates, the man who owned the house she stayed in brought her a fine, fat sea trout. "Joan, stop a moment," he said. "Let us eat this fish before you go."

"Leave it for this evening," she answered. "We will have it for supper. I will bring you back an Englishman to share it with us. And tonight," she added, "I will come back by way of the bridge."

No Frenchman had crossed that bridge since Captain Glasdale had taken les Tourelles. The French leaders, even those who admired Joan, did not believe anyone would cross it that day either. They felt that another assault across the river would serve only to provoke a counterattack by the English. The Lord of Gaucourt, who guarded the Gate of Burgundy with his host of retainers, tried to hold back the townsfolk who had armed themselves and were following Joan through the streets. He warned that attacking the English again would cost many lives.

"Whether you wish it or not," cried Joan, "our soldiers will come and will win, as they have won before." And standing in her stirrups, she shouted, "Let who loves me follow me." A mighty roar went up from the crowd, and Gaucourt was compelled to order the gate opened and let them pass through.

Les Tourelles was a small fortress but difficult to get at. On its south side the English had dug a deep ditch to protect the bridgehead. Behind the ditch was a barricade called an outwork, and a drawbridge connected the outwork with the main fortress itself. On the north side—the side facing Orléans—the English were protected mainly by the gap made when the French had damaged the bridge. The English had thrown up a low wall of rubble to provide further cover for archers on their side of the gap.

The French focused their attack on the south side of the fortress—against the ditch below the outwork. Again and again they climbed down into the ditch, trying to scale the outwork or perhaps breach it. They were driven back, each time, by a hail of arrows.

"They fought," says a chronicler, "as if they were immortal, but many were wounded and killed." And Joan stayed among them, in the front line all the time, to cheer them on. The English showed no signs of weakness, however, for they fought back stubbornly with axes and mallets, as well as guns and pikes. Some of them used their bare hands. By late afternoon the French seemed to be weakening. Joan, determined as ever, placed a ladder against the wall, as though she would lead her troops over the wall despite the opposition. She had no sooner set foot on the lowest rung when her prophecy was fulfilled: she was hit by an enemy arrow.

Coming from above, the arrow struck that unprotected part of her shoulder, close by her neck, where the breastplate ended. She had chosen not to wear a helmet so she would always be easy to recognize. Thus, her neck and head were bare.

From Dunois' account, it appears that the arrow pierced the muscle above Joan's collarbone and went in far enough to emerge from the back of her shoulder. The impact of the shot hurled her to the ground. She lay there only a moment, for Jean de Gamache, the knight who had once wanted to give up his banner rather than serve her, was suddenly by her side.

"Take my horse," he said, as he lifted her to her feet. He apologized for his former rudeness, and she replied, "I have never seen a knight so nobly bred," and she assured him she did not bear a grudge against him.

The English cheered as Joan was helped from the battlefield; the French, on their side, were disheartened. They continued to throw themselves valiantly against the outwork but could not overcome it.

Meanwhile, Joan was taken half-fainting to a quiet meadow. She was frightened by the pain she felt and by the sight of her own blood. But the fear that she could not continue the fight and that les Tourelles might not be stormed made her weep. The honor of her countrymen depended on her; she felt she had let them down.

Her friends were around her now. One of them cut off the iron tip of the arrow, and it is said that Joan herself pulled out the shaft. The wound was painful, though not serious, but had the arrow entered at a slightly different angle, it doubtless would have killed her. "I have been comforted," Joan said when her wound had been dressed with fat and oil and the blood had ceased to flow. She felt weak and dizzy, but she struggled to her feet. Donning her armor once more, Joan returned to the attack.

She was in the thick of the battle when Dunois reluctantly decided to order a retreat. It was eight o'clock in the evening;

the troops, who had struggled for thirteen hours in vain attacks, were exhausted. But before the trumpets could sound, Joan went to Dunois and asked for more time. "In God's name, do not retreat," she begged him. "You will enter the place soon. Fear nothing, and the English will have no power over you."

Knowing how tired his soldiers were, Dunois hesitated, but Joan went on passionately, persuasively: "When you see my standard fluttering out and pointing toward the fort, resume your arms again and [the fortress] shall be yours." If the soldiers are weary, she said, they should be allowed first to "eat and drink to refresh themselves."

To this Dunois agreed. And while the men sprawled about, relieving their weariness and munching bread and cheese, Joan rode up the hill to a nearby vineyard where she spent about a quarter of an hour in prayer. The men could see her there, standing alone, a small, sturdy figure with her face upturned, the last light of day shining on her armor.

Meanwhile, according to the account he later gave, Joan's squire had conceived of a worthy and chivalrous deed. Afraid that if the French actually retreated, the English would attack and destroy them, d'Aulon decided that Joan was right: the assault on les Tourelles had to be continued. If only Joan's white standard could be carried forward, perhaps the men would be inspired to make one last drive to victory.

The standard, which she had left behind, had been given to

a brave and powerfully built man-at-arms called the Basque. D'Aulon reported the following:

> *I asked the Basque whether if I were to run toward the foot of the bulwark he would follow me, and he promised to do so. Then I leaped into the ditch and came under the bulwark wall, covering myself with my shield for fear of stones, and certain that my companion would follow close after me.*

But the Basque had been intercepted. Joan, returning from the vineyard, had seen her precious standard being carried away, and thinking it had been stolen, had run forward to retrieve it. She tried to pull it away from the Basque, but he held fast, remembering his promise to d'Aulon. Joan was stunned by what happened next. For the French captains, seeing the Maid's standard waving to and fro, believed this was the signal to advance. They ordered the men to their feet, quickly reassembled them, and sent them charging off toward the outwork.

Joan understood now, and she shouted to the troops, "All is yours. Take the wall!" Nothing could stop them. French men-at-arms raced up their ladders, knocked out the English resistance at the top of the wall, and soon were pouring over the barrier.

Meanwhile, other French troops were streaming out of Orléans with reinforcements and a makeshift wooden bridge to span the gap in the stone bridge just north of les Tourelles. The wooden bridge was put in place, and a number of soldiers raced across it, single file, to attack the barrier the English had raised. Others loaded an old barge with pitch, olive oil, and grease-soaked rags and rowed it underneath the drawbridge that separated the outwork on the south shore from the castle of les Tourelles. When the barge was in position, the French set fire to it and leaped to the safety of the bank. The boat's incendiary cargo fed the flames until the blaze spread to the drawbridge overhead.

Now Captain Glasdale had to retreat to les Tourelles. He and about a score of his knights stood off the French while several hundred of his archers and men-at-arms got back across the drawbridge. Then the sound of Joan's voice could be heard above the din of battle. "Glasdale, Glasdale," she called, "surrender to the King of Heaven. You have called me strumpet, but I have pity on your soul and the souls of your men."

Neither Glasdale nor his companions replied. They were knights, and they preferred death to the dishonor of surrendering to a woman—particularly one they thought to be wicked. They turned and dashed across the drawbridge on the heels of their men. But the beams had been weakened by the fire, and the smoldering bridge collapsed beneath them. They plunged like stones into the river; the weight of their armor dragged them to the bottom.

Several hours after nightfall the Maid returned to Orléans, her path lighted by hundreds of torches. The city was a riot of ringing bells and shouting voices, and the priests and towns-folk all sang hymns of thanksgiving.

Early the next day, watchmen on the walls of the city reported that English troops were marching out of their western fortresses, the only strongholds left to them. Joan put on a light coat of mail—her wound prevented her from wearing her breastplate—and rode with Dunois and La Hire through the city's western gate. Seeing her, some soldiers asked, "Today being Sunday, is it wrong to fight?" And she replied, "If they attack you, defend yourselves and they will be yours."

Priests came forth and in the open air said mass. When the service was finished, the Maid was heard to ask, "What are the English doing? Do you see their faces or their backs?" She was told that the English were marching away. They were with-drawing, even though Fastolf and his army were presumably on the way to bolster them.

"Let them depart in peace," the Maid said. "You will get them another time." A great shout of joy went up. Orléans was saved; the first of Joan's great tasks had been accomplished.

CHAPTER 7

A STRING OF VICTORIES

JOAN HAD MADE THREE PROMISES TO THE Dauphin. She said she would relieve the siege of Orléans, take him to Reims to be anointed and crowned, and expel the English at last from France. Now that the first of these promises had been fulfilled, Joan began trying to achieve the second. But circumstances and people seemed allied against her.

First of all, to reach Reims the French would have to pass through territory in which nearly all the cities and towns were under English or Burgundian control. And second, the Dauphin's own advisers were opposed to Joan's plans. Each of these men, for reasons of his own, was determined to delay, and if possible forestall, everything the Maid tried to do. However they may have disagreed on other matters, they were united in their displeasure at having a seventeen-year-old country girl win the adoration of the French people and gain the Dauphin's favor. Of course they were eager to see Charles crowned king—but not just yet, only after their individual objectives had been achieved.

Some of the nobles believed that troops should be sent to Normandy, where the people were known to be growing restless under the English yoke. Others were convinced that a peace treaty with Burgundy should be attempted. The Maid was staunchly opposed to both of these plans. Pressure was being exerted to make Joan change her mind, but her determination could not be shaken. Reims was her objective, and to make sure that the Dauphin shared her purpose, she decided to go and talk to him herself.

The citizens of Orléans wept when she left them. On May 9, only ten days after her arrival, she rode out of the city, and the people pressed around her, kissing her hands and feet and offering her gifts and servants.

She rode to meet Charles, who was on his way from Chinon to Tours. She could hardly contain her joy as she saw him riding toward her. When she was abreast of him, Joan raised her steel cap and bowed low over her horse's neck. Charles took off his hat and embraced her. It was perhaps the only gesture of tenderness that he ever made to her; he would never express any gratitude.

She rode into Tours by his side and then waited impatiently while he met with his council. She could not understand the delay. Nor could she know that her "gentle Dauphin" was in a dilemma, which she had caused indirectly. For the miraculous freeing of Orléans had been achieved in less than two weeks, ending a six-month siege. Now what was the Dauphin to do? No plans had been made beyond Orléans. He was as befuddled in victory as he had always been in defeat.

More than two weeks passed while Joan waited and fretted. One day, accompanied by Dunois, she went to the royal chamber where the Dauphin was in conference with his nobles. She knocked and entered boldly. Falling to her knees, she embraced Charles' feet.

"Noble Dauphin," she began, "do not spend so much time in council, but come with me at once to Reims to be crowned." Immediately a bishop asked her if her own counsel—that is, her voices—had advised her to say this. She replied that indeed they had, and that they had become most pressing.

"Will you not tell us," said the bishop, "what manner of counsel it is which thus speaks to you?"

Joan blushed, and for a moment she hesitated. "I understand well what you want to know," she said finally, "and I will gladly tell you." The Dauphin, noting her hesitation, said gently, "Joan, does it please you to answer this question before all of us?"

"Yes, Sire," she answered. Dunois, remembering that scene later, said:

She told us . . . that when something was not going well . . . she would retire apart and pray to God, complaining to Him that the men to whom she spoke would not believe her. And when she had prayed, she heard a voice which said, "Go, Daughter of God, go, and I will help you!" And when she heard this voice she felt a great joy and wished she could always be in this happy state. And what is more, when she thus repeated to us the words of her voices, she was seized with a marvelous rapture and raised her eyes to heaven.

It may be that this interview spurred Charles to action. He had always been impressed by Joan's own knowledge that her time was limited. For earlier she had urged him, "Use me. I will last only a little more than a year. During that year let as much as possible be done." It was her impatience now, more than her words, that Charles understood and believed. He concluded he must do as she insisted.

It was decided, however, that the many English strongholds along the Loire, near Orléans, would have to be taken before the French could march to Reims. A new army was organized and brought together at Orléans. Joan re-entered that city on June 9 and rested there for just two days before setting out for the nearby city of Jargeau. With her were some eight thousand men and a host of captains, including La Hire, Alençon, and Dunois.

A month before, soon after the siege of Orléans had ended, Dunois had tried to capture Jargeau on his own. He had done some damage, but in the end he had been forced to retreat. Now Joan was to show her power.

Jargeau was held by no more than two thousand English troops, led by the Earl of Suffolk and his two gallant brothers, John and Alexander Pole. The walls of the city were strong, and its English garrison was heartened by a rumor that Sir John Fastolf was on his way with supplies and reinforcements.

A wave of uncertainty swept through the French ranks, for Fastolf was an enemy the French still feared. Since he had been heading for Orléans before the siege was lifted, it was assumed that he was somewhere nearby. Some of Joan's captains suggested that Fastolf be intercepted, but she said no. "Do not fear, no matter how numerous the enemy may be," she assured them, "and do not hesitate to assault these English, since God has this work in hand."

The French headed straight for Jargeau and reached the outskirts of the city on June 11. Suffolk himself met them, leading his men-at-arms in a desperate charge, for he hoped to avert an attack on the city. Utterly surprised, the French were repulsed at first, but the Maid galloped forward, shouting, "At them! At them!" Seeing her standard, the soldiers fought back savagely. Suffolk and his men were forced to retreat to the city, and the French made their camp in the suburbs that night.

The next day Suffolk offered a truce that would last two weeks, promising to surrender at the end of that time if relief had not reached him. He felt certain that Fastolf would arrive by then. But the French captains, urged on by Joan, would not hear of it. Although Joan abhorred needless bloodshed, she considered a conditional surrender no surrender at all. "The English may leave Jargeau in their armor, with their lives," she said. "If they will not, the town shall be stormed."

The Duke of Alençon hesitated. He feared that it might be too soon to launch an attack. "Fear nothing," said the Maid. "Go forward, and God will prepare the way. Do you not know I promised your wife I would bring you back safe and sound?" On this, he ordered his trumpets to sound the assault and went off to lead his troops against the walls.

The battle was brief and hot. In the midst of it, seeing a small cannon being aimed from the wall, Joan cried out to Alençon, "Move aside!" He obeyed her instinctively, and moments later, on that very spot, a knight was killed by the same cannon. During the melee, Joan herself was struck. Holding her standard, she had begun to climb a ladder when a stone ricocheted off her standard and hit the light steel cap she was wearing. The cap was knocked off, and Joan was thrown to the ground. It was a terrifying moment for the French, for they were afraid she had been crushed by the blow. But she scrambled to her feet in an instant, shouting, "Up, friends, up! The English are ours!" And the wall was scaled.

Suffolk and his brothers were unable to escape. John was captured, Alexander slain. And Suffolk, completely surrounded, was fighting for his life. Suddenly he turned to a French squire, the nearest of his enemies, and asked him to kneel and accept the formal sword tap, or "accolade," of knighthood. Not until that ceremony had been completed could the young man, now a full-fledged knight, receive Suffolk's surrender. The rest of the English garrison then dropped their weapons. Jargeau had fallen.

Meung, downriver from Orléans, was next. The bridge was seized, but the town was not stormed. Then the French marched on Beaugency, which surrendered without a fight. But the very morning on which the garrison was withdrawing, a French man-at-arms ran breathlessly to the Duke of Alençon, warning him, "The English are marching upon us!"

It was Sir John Fastolf and Lord Talbot, with their combined army of thousands. Fastolf had agreed to join Talbot in support of the English garrison at Beaugency, but neither man knew that the town had already capitulated. When they came within a few miles of it they halted, for the French army could be seen across the plain, arrayed on the top of a hill. The

English deployed into their customary defensive position behind a stockade of wooden stakes jabbed into the earth, their points tilted toward the enemy. The longbowmen stood behind this barricade, poised and waiting.

Meanwhile, the French leaders watched from the hilltop. When the sun was low in the sky, Alençon asked Joan what she thought should be done now. "See that you have good spurs," she answered.

"What?" asked the Duke. "Are we to turn our backs on them and flee?"

"No," said Joan, "they will be beaten. You will need good spurs to chase them."

But there was no fighting that evening, and by the time the sun rose the next day, the English had gone. They had broken camp and marched off toward Janville and the road to Paris. Now, indeed, the French made use of their "good spurs" and set out at once. Joan said that "if they were hanging from the clouds, we should still catch them. This very day our King will win a greater victory than ever before."

The English withdrew to a spot near the town of Patay. They reined in their horses and prepared an ambush. Talbot placed his guns and the heavy carts of his wagon train along the edge of a forest. A detachment of troops was entrenched behind this barricade. The main body took up a position in a hidden valley. Five hundred archers were stationed behind hedges along the road leading into the valley. Talbot had used the topography to form a trap, and he was sure his enemy would ride directly into it.

While the English lay hidden, French scouts were riding to look for them. Suddenly a stag darted out of a thicket, frightened by the sound of approaching horses. It zigzagged down the road toward the valley, past the hedges where the bowmen were concealed.

The love of sport got the best of the English thirst for combat—for what man who called himself an archer could resist a shot at a stag? The English, unaware that French scouts were nearby, loosed their shafts at the game, whistling and whooping in their excitement. Immediately a scout was sent back to the French captains with word that the quarry had been found.

What happened next took place so quickly, so violently, and in such confusion that it is almost impossible to know the details. First, a vanguard of French cavalry swept up, following the scouts, and cut the unsuspecting English archers to pieces before they could even draw their bows. In terror, Fastolf and most of the troops he commanded ran off toward the forest. He hoped, no doubt, to take shelter behind the wagons, just as he had done with success at the Battle of the Herrings. But the men there, seeing him come so fast and with the French banners so close behind him, thought all was lost and scattered at once into the woods.

The battle was over in a matter of minutes. By the time Joan and the main body of French troops arrived on the scene, there was hardly any need for them to strike a blow. Two thousand English archers and men-at-arms were slain, and more than a thousand were captured. Sir John Fastolf managed to escape, but Lord Talbot was taken prisoner. He was brought before Alençon, who could not resist saying, "This morning you little thought that you would be a prisoner of war by this afternoon."

"It is the fortune of war," Talbot replied grimly. Fortune had now tipped the balance to the side of the French. The Battle of Patay, as this triumph came to be called, had made up amply for the long string of past English victories.

CHAPTER 8

JOAN'S SECOND MISSION: TO CROWN A KING

NOW, JOAN WAS MORE DETERMINED THAN EVER to complete her second great task, the march to Reims for Charles' coronation. Though the Dauphin's councilors still opposed her, she at last had her way. And at least as far as the great mass of French people were concerned, she was right. To them Charles was no more than a prince until he had been formally crowned and anointed. The English themselves understood the importance of this act, for they had taken the crown of Charlemagne from Reims, along with other royal symbols and the enamel and silver-gilt book that contained the coronation ritual. The English intended to use these objects of royalty for the formal crowning of young Henry VI as king of France. But for the French, these objects were not so significant as the service of coronation and the place itself.

The place, Reims, was the city where, in 496, Saint Rémy had baptized and anointed King Clovis, the first Christian king of France. Since that time, the kings of France had been anointed and had received their crowns there. Did not the Bible describe how the prophet Samuel had poured oil on the head of Saul, the first king of Israel, saying, "Is it not because the Lord hath anointed thee to be captain over his inheritance"?

According to the legend, Clovis had been thus anointed with oil that had been brought from heaven to Saint Rémy by a white dove. This same oil was still in Reims, retained in a crystal flask, and it was believed that the amount of oil in the flask never varied—no matter how often it was used.

Reims lay deep in the English-held region of Champagne; thus the French would have to fight to get there. The first city of importance along their route was Auxerre, and it was here that La Tremoïlle, Charles' chief adviser, demonstrated his method of making war. Joan wanted to assault Auxerre, but La Tremoïlle accepted a bribe of two thousand gold pieces from the burgesses in exchange for a promise not to attack. The city surrendered, and the French army moved on to Troyes.

After two days of siege, that city opened its gates, although its leaders had sworn never to submit to the Dauphin. A few days later, Châlons also surrendered, and its Anglo-Burgundian garrison, like that of Troyes, was permitted to march away. When the army reached Reims, the Burgundian captain of the garrison offered to hold the city against the French, but the citizens refused the offer and prepared to welcome the Dauphin. In desperation, the captain tried to steal the holy oil, but he failed and fled to join the English.

Charles VII entered Reims on July 16, 1429, with Joan and his barons and princes behind him. The masters of the guilds, the journeymen, the merchants—all with the banners and emblems of their crafts—and masses of citizens flocked to greet the royal party. At nine o'clock the next morning, Charles entered the cathedral. Joan stood by his side with her standard unfurled. There was a long wait while a procession of monks and canons from the Abbey of Saint Rémy walked slowly through the streets, bearing the holy oil. At the cathedral doors, the flask was handed over to the archbishop, Regnault of Chartres, who carried it to the altar.

From his cousin, Alençon, Charles received the belt and spurs of chivalry. With his head covered and his hand upon the Gospels, he swore to defend the Church, to banish heretics, and to preserve his people and govern them with justice and mercy. "This I say and swear by oath," he declared.

The barons placed about his shoulders a blue mantle flowered with golden lilies. They girded a sword to his side and gave him the scepter and the rod of justice. The archbishop took the crystal flask, and with some oil on his fingertips made the sign of the cross on Charles' forehead. "I consecrate thee," he said, "with this holy oil in the name of the Father, the Son, and the Holy Ghost."

A crown was placed on Charles' head. It was not the ancient crown of Charlemagne, resplendent with rubies and sapphires, but a more modest one provided by the canons of the cathedral. Charles rose to his feet, no longer the Dauphin, but King of France. He was led to the throne, while in the great vault of the church the voice of the archbishop echoed, "Long live the King!"

The barons repeated the cry, and the church reverberated to the shouts of *"Noël! Noël!"* from the audience. Trumpets sounded, and the doors were swung wide. Hordes of people were gathered outside in the cathedral square, waiting to see their monarch.

Joan knelt, sobbing with joy. "Fair King," she said, "now is God's will done, and you have received your holy anointing, showing that you are the true king and lord over the land of France."

Reims was the scene of jubilation on that warm summer Sunday. At last France had a king again. The country seemed to be emerging from the suffocating embrace of the Hundred Years' War.

For the knights, the men-at-arms, and the people who lived in Reims, it was a day of hope and optimism. There was feasting everywhere. For a farmer named Jacques d'Arc, who had come to the city, it was a day of joy and boundless pride. When his daughter left home, only five months before, she was wearing a patched dress. Now she wore gleaming armor, a cloak of crimson and gold, and she stood beside the King. Jacques himself was presented to Charles and was given a fine gift for his fellow villagers in Domrémy: freedom from paying taxes.

For Joan it was a day of triumph. Everyone in Reims seemed to know that a peasant girl had relieved the siege of Orléans and had brought Charles to his coronation. She could not pass through the streets without provoking a demonstration; people longed to see her, to touch her, to kiss the hem of her cloak. They marveled at her appearance: a slight girl, however strong, and shy, however bold. "Do you really fight?" one of them asked her. "Are you not afraid?"

"I am afraid of nothing but treachery," she said. She may have suspected the intrigue that was even then being carried on behind her back.

CHAPTER 9

THE KING HESITATES AT THE WALLS OF PARIS

IT WAS IMPERATIVE TO JOAN THAT CHARLES should now march on Paris. Since he held a strong military advantage, she expected him to order his army to capture the capital. But instead Charles waited, and vacillated. The days passed, and Joan became impatient. She knew her time was growing short.

Some chroniclers suggest that Charles turned away from Joan when he became king and that he believed he no longer needed her. There are also indications that as king he felt he should not allow a peasant girl still in her teens to continue influencing his actions and decisions. Perhaps he would have been pleased if Joan had decided her heaven-sent mission was over and had bid him farewell. Instead she continued to exert pressure on him; so did his councilors. And the pressure was getting intense.

The royal council, notably Regnault of Chartres and La Tremoïlle, took a cautious view of things. They wanted the King to enter Paris but were in no hurry. For some time, La Tremoïlle had been working quietly and resolutely to achieve an accord with Duke Philip of Burgundy. Paris was a Burgundian stronghold. If La Tremoïlle succeeded in having the city given up peacefully to France, he, rather than the Maid, would gain the credit.

Joan also recognized that the best way to gain Paris was to break up the Anglo-Burgundian alliance. A full three weeks before the coronation, she had sent a letter to Duke Philip— but, unlike La Tremoïlle, Joan insisted that the Duke honor the sovereignty of King Charles.

In blunt language she urged Burgundy to attend the ceremony and take his place among the other noblemen at the high altar. As he did not reply, Joan sent another letter, on the day of the crowning, saying:

Joan the Maid, in the name of the King of Heaven, requires you and the King of France to make a good and lasting peace . . . Forgive one another entirely as becomes good Christians, and if you must make war, go against the Saracens. Prince of Burgundy, I pray you, I entreat you as humbly as I can not to make war any longer against the holy realm of France, and speedily to withdraw your men from the strongholds and fortresses of the said holy kingdom; as for the King of France, he is ready to make any peace with you that will satisfy honor . . .

While Joan's letter was on its way to Duke Philip a delegation of his ambassadors was arriving in Reims. It is probable that Joan did not know this; King Charles' royal councilors were doing their best to keep her ignorant of their deliberations. In any case, she would have been extremely suspicious of the offer made by the Burgundian representatives, for it was a curious one indeed.

Burgundy promised to surrender Paris to the King—but only after a two-week period of truce—an agreement that did not please Joan, when she finally learned of it. Her distress and disappointment were expressed in a letter she later sent to the town council of Reims. The letter said in part:

I am not in favor of truces made in this way, and I do not know whether I will keep it; but if I do keep it, it will only be to preserve the King's honor, that the royal blood should suffer no harm. For I will keep the King's army together in readiness, lest at the end of the fifteen days they should not make peace.

The royal council did not share Joan's anxiety. Philip's offer was tentatively accepted after three or four days' debate. About two weeks later, the King signed the agreement. He had left Reims soon after the coronation, leading his army through English-held territory along the Aisne River to receive the submission of a number of towns and cities. Everywhere he went he was hailed in triumphal processions, and people offered him gifts and pledged allegiance to him.

Charles had been lulled by his advisers into thinking that he could topple his enemies, Bedford and Burgundy, through negotiation and peaceful surrender. Joan pleaded her case with him, urging him not to let his army stagnate, but he seemed not to hear her. And some said that Joan had lost her divine powers, that not even her voices spoke to her anymore. Actually, her voices were becoming more and more insistent. "Daughter of God—onward, onward, onward!" they urged her, and the more her wishes were stifled or ignored, the more certain she was that treachery was being plotted against her.

Her distrust of Duke Philip was well founded, of course, for long before he made the truce with Charles, he had agreed to help the English defend Paris. In exchange, Bedford had promised him great sums of money. Clearly, Philip's offer of a two-week truce had been a device for gaining time. For while he was negotiating with France, a force of four thousand fresh English troops was on its way across the Channel to Normandy. By the time the unsuspecting Charles had signed the treaty, Bedford himself had arrived to take command of this force and was leading it to the south.

In early August Charles and his army were also moving south. Many people believed the King was retreating, and this caused panic in the towns that had offered homage and obeisance to him. With the French army gone, they were vulnerable to reprisals by the English. But Charles' journey south was probably not a retreat. It is believed he was trying to secure the region that lay between Reims and the Loire: he could not consider taking Paris, by force or surrender, while there was still so much hostile territory around it.

He crossed the Marne, receiving the keys to half a dozen towns, and then continued south until he reached the river Seine. Here an obstacle halted him. A force of English had seized the bridge over the river and cut off his route. Many of the French knights believed the bridgehead could be taken, but Joan for one was glad Charles declined to try it. She had opposed his decision to cross the Seine and was pleased that he was being forced to turn north again. Marching north meant moving closer to Paris, which was her goal.

The Duke of Bedford had grown perplexed and annoyed by Charles' random movements. By the time the French army had recrossed the Marne, a letter had been dispatched to the King, which began:

We, John of Lancaster, Regent of France and Duke of Bedford, make known to you, Charles of Valois, who . . . at present without cause call yourself king, for wrongfully do you make attempts against the crown of the high, excellent, and renowned Prince Henry . . . deceiving the simple people by telling them you come to give peace and security, which cannot be done by the means you have pursued and are now following to seduce and abuse ignorant people, with the aid of superstitious and damnable persons such as a woman of a disorderly and infamous life and dissolute manners dressed in the clothes of a man . . .

From this beginning, almost incoherently insulting, Bedford went on to challenge the King either to meet him and his army in combat "in any competent place" or come forward with a proposal for peace. Even apathetic Charles was stung by the arrogance of this letter. He is said to have cried, "Bedford need not look for me. I will search him out myself!"

On August 13 the two armies were approaching each other near the town of Montepilloy. Neither Charles nor Bedford seemed eager to enter a full-scale encounter. For after two days of skirmishing between opposing outposts and patrols, the armies separated without ever engaging in a general battle.

Bedford marched off into Normandy to strengthen the English positions there, and Charles sent Regnault of Chartres to

73

the Duke of Burgundy to request another peace treaty. Charles was concerned because the two-week truce had expired and Paris still showed no signs of surrender. When Regnault returned, he reported that nothing had been concluded, but the Duke had agreed to send ambassadors to King Charles to confer further on the subject. And Charles retired some fifty miles north of Paris to Compiègne, which surrendered peacefully. He did not indicate whether he would attempt any further action.

No doubt Joan fretted and fumed at the King's passive attitude, for she had warned that there would be no peace save at the point of the lance. Finally she could stand it no longer. "My fair Duke," she said to Alençon, "command your men to arm. I must go to Paris!" On August 23, with a picked company following them, Joan and Alençon set out.

They rode to St. Denis, seven miles north of Paris. This was one of the country's oldest and most important towns, for in its abbey the kings of France were buried. St. Denis opened its gates to Joan and Alençon, and an adoring crowd followed wherever they went. They reconnoitered the walls of Paris, discussed how that city might be taken, and sent urgent pleas to King Charles to join them at St. Denis. But Charles was busy. On August 28 he signed another treaty with Burgundy.

This one was even more peculiar than the first. It extended the truce until Christmas and, among other things, gave Duke

Philip the right to defend Paris and "to resist such as shall make war upon it or do hurt." But it did not forbid the King from trying to recover his capital, and repeatedly Alençon went to Charles, urging him to adopt this course. Finally the King agreed.

During the long period of France's division, Paris had sided with the Burgundians against the crown. Now rumors swept through the city that Charles intended to take it and would give it over to fire and pillage and plow up the very ground on which it stood. In vain the Duke of Alençon wrote soothing letters to the burgesses to assure them that no harm would come to Paris.

The King arrived at St. Denis on September 7, and on that day Joan was involved in an incident that cast a pall of gloom on the royal army. From her first contact with the troops, Joan had called upon them to give up cursing, thievery, and consorting with loose women. Many of them had obeyed her, but many had not—and had chosen to take their women along with them wherever they went. A number of these wenches were dressed in armor to avoid being identified. At St. Denis the Maid ordered several of these women to leave the camp. One of them refused; enraged, Joan struck her with the flat of her sword. The blade snapped in two.

Joan insisted that this was not the sword that had come from the Church of St. Catherine. But it was whispered among the troops that the sword she had broken was indeed that holy weapon. It was also believed that the King himself had said to Joan, "You should have used a stick rather than the sword given you by heaven." Many were now convinced that the Maid had lost her power.

Added to this unhappy augury was the fact that the attack on Paris was begun on a holy day, the Feast of the Nativity of the Virgin, September 8. Though that was but a small sin amidst the mass violence and cruelty of war, it would later be counted against Joan. And as though doomed by its portentous beginning, the entire assault was marked by confusion, halfheartedness, and incompetence. The choice of the day was only one more bad omen.

The French had thrown a bridge across the Seine on the south side of Paris a few days before, evidently with the idea of assaulting the city from two sides. But no one used this bridge. There was only one assault, and it was directed against the Gate of St. Honoré on the north side of the city.

The attack began at noon as French soldiers set fire to the wooden barrier that had been erected in front of St. Honoré. The first obstacle had been overcome. But there were others— a long dry trench at least ten feet deep, a mound of earth, and a water-filled moat more than sixty feet wide that followed the line of the city walls. The French swarmed across the dry trench and up on the earthen mound. The moat lay before them, but none of the chiefs of war had figured out just how they were going to cross it.

Joan's army had equipment for most contingencies, but this time rafts had not been included in the siege train. To make up for the lack, the French gathered bundles of fagots to fill in the moat so it could be crossed. This method might have worked splendidly in a few feet of water, but the moat before the walls of Paris was too deep; the fagots simply floated away. From their side, the French could do little more than exchange arrows with English soldiers perched on top of the walls. Meanwhile, the Maid went along the edge of the moat, sounding the depth of the water with her lance in the hope of finding a shallow spot.

While she was doing so, a bolt from an enemy crossbow struck her on the thigh. It must have hit the armor squarely, for it split the steel plate. The bolt entered Joan's flesh—not deeply, but enough so that she was in great pain and could not remain standing. An instant later another bolt pierced the foot of the young page who carried her standard. He raised his visor, perhaps so he could see to pull the bolt free, and a second one caught him between the eyes. He fell dead, and Joan's white standard dropped to the ground.

Joan was carried to shelter behind the mound, but she refused to leave the battle. She called to the men to go forward and take the walls; yet the afternoon dragged on to darkness, and the French had not crossed the water. At ten o'clock that evening the French finally gave up. Two knights bore Joan from the field, much against her will. "In God's name," she cried, "the city might have been ours!"

Despite her wound, Joan had herself placed in the saddle the next day. She started toward Paris once again with Alençon at her side and the soldiers behind her. Their spirits were lifted; a new assault was in the making. They felt hopeful that because the Seine had been bridged, they still had a chance to enter Paris. But Charles also knew of that bridge, and during the night he had ordered it destroyed. Then, before any other move could be planned, he sent orders for the troops to return to St. Denis.

Why was Charles being so cautious? Possibly he still hoped to gain Paris peacefully by making an agreement with Burgundy. Or possibly his advisers had increased their pressure on him not to fight. Whatever the reason, the royal army withdrew from St. Denis three days later without striking another blow. King Charles was returning to his castles in the Loire Valley.

Before accompanying him, Joan went to the Cathedral of St. Denis; there, as a votive offering, she hung before the image of the Virgin the armor she had worn at Paris. The armor was said to be black now, as if Joan were already in mourning for the fate that was to come.

CHAPTER 10

JOAN'S THIRD MISSION FAILS

AT THE TIME OF HIS CORONATION, KING CHARLES had nearly ten thousand armed men led by seasoned knights and inspired by the Maid, who had made them feel invincible. Victory was within his grasp then, but he allowed it to slip away. If his troops had gone to Paris the day after his anointing, and if they had surrounded the city and assaulted it with all their strength, Charles might have entered the capital in triumph. Or, when confronted by Bedford at Montepilloy, if Charles had sent the Maid forward with his army, the English might have been defeated.

But the young King was never one to act firmly or decisively, and he could not change now, no matter how hard Joan tried to put heart into him. The belief that peaceful diplomacy could settle all that was still unsolved reinforced his desire to fight no more. Since Burgundy seemed willing to negotiate, why antagonize him by provoking more warfare? That thought seemed to be foremost in Charles' mind.

So he turned his back on the military advantages that had been won for him, and after the disastrous attempt to take Paris, he traveled southward. At Bourges, while his army disintegrated, he took up the courtly life from which Joan had plucked him six months prior. La Hire, with his usual candor, had once said of Charles, "I have never seen a prince lose his estates so gaily." If La Hire had been in Bourges, his voice might have joined with Joan's to make a noise the King would have heard.

But La Hire was in Normandy, winning away lands from the English. The Duke of Alençon, seeing that nothing more could be done in the region around Paris, made plans to go to Maine to regain some of his holdings there. He begged the King to let Joan accompany him, but Charles refused. Alençon rode away alone; Joan and her "fair Duke" were never to meet again.

Joan spent much of her time during the next few months in La Tremoïlle's castle at Sully on the Loire. Here, it was suspected, she was almost a prisoner. Her dream of taking Paris one day was finally demolished when she heard that the King had signed still another truce with the Duke of Burgundy. This one guaranteed that the French attack on Paris would not be renewed. Nevertheless, Joan urged that her services be put to use, and eventually she was ordered to put on her armor. It was not the King, but La Tremoïlle and others on the royal council, who wanted her to fight—and for their own purposes.

Two small towns in the Loire district still continued to be rebellious, and the council decided that the resistance should be put down. An army was assembled, and Joan rode at the head of the troops. The first town to be assaulted was St. Pierre-le-Moustier, which was defended by a company of English and Burgundian men-at-arms who were known for their brutality. After two days of fighting, the attack was beaten back, and the French troops retreated to their camp. There Joan's squire, d'Aulon, learned that the Maid had not yet returned. Her absence troubled him, though he had worries of his own. He had been wounded in the foot and was hobbling about on crutches, but he mounted his horse and rode back to get her.

D'Aulon found Joan standing at the edge of the moat outside the town with no more than half a dozen men around her. "What are you doing here alone?" he cried. She pulled off her steel cap and looked about. "I am not alone," she insisted. "There are fifty thousand of my folk with me. I will not leave this spot until the town is taken."

Ignoring her reference to supernatural forces at her command, d'Aulon pleaded with Joan. "Come with me. Come back to camp with the others." But she would not. "Bring bundles of fagots," she shouted. "Let us bridge the moat."

A few of the men ran back to camp to fetch the others, and a fresh attack was begun. The moat was bridged, and before the day ended the town had fallen.

Now the French moved on to La Charité-sur-Loire, a town on the Loire not far north of St. Pierre. Although it was of some importance strategically, La Charité-sur-Loire was even more important to La Tremoïlle personally.

The town had been seized from France five years before by a hard-bitten Burgundian captain named Perrinet Gressart. In the winter of that year, 1425, he had taken La Tremoïlle prisoner and held him for a ransom of fourteen thousand gold crowns. The ransom was paid, and La Tremoïlle bore a grudge that grew more intense with the passing years. He thought primarily of revenge against Gressart when he sent Joan to La Charité-sur-Loire.

The siege began in bitter November weather and did not proceed well. Soon the besiegers found themselves in need of provisions and short of money to pay the men-at-arms. Casualties increased as the royal army tried repeatedly to penetrate the town. But the Burgundians fought hard. Gressart, a wily soldier, had assured his men that the Maid had no sorcery to help her except their own fear of her. On moonless nights he had trumpets blown while his men cheered so that the French would think a steady stream of reinforcements was pouring in. The French leaders, convinced they could not long hold out against Gressart, decided to pull back. If Joan protested, they overruled her; the French retired to Bourges, abandoning much of their equipment. Their retreat was all the more disgraceful because Gressart had no chance of being relieved, and eventually he would have had to surrender.

Joan indicated later that she had received no heavenly guidance at La Charité-sur-Loire. She never said her voices had forbidden her to fight there, but her failure to take the town strengthened the growing belief that her counsel had abandoned her. Indeed her position had changed now. From being a leader sent by God to bring victory, she had become a kind of mascot. And though she insisted she had one more task—to expel the English from France—she was no nearer to accomplishing it.

The winter dragged on, and Duke Philip of Burgundy continued his negotiations for peace with King Charles. While these overtures were being made, Philip worked behind the scenes to arouse popular feeling in towns not yet committed either to him or to Charles. When a Burgundian force moved menacingly close to Reims, Joan dictated a note of encouragement to the citizens. The message was dated March 28, 1430, and it said: "Hold the city well for the King, and keep good watch. You will soon have good word of me at greater length."

Soon after sending the note she gathered together a hundred riders and some seventy archers and crossbowmen. With this force, and an Italian knight named Bartolomeo Baretta to lead it, Joan and her squire headed north. Some historians believe she pretended to be going on a military exercise, hoping she could lure the King to follow her to war once again. It is more likely, however, that the royal council had asked her to prepare for battle because the truce with Burgundy was about to expire. Whatever the reason, when she departed from Charles, it was for the last time.

CHAPTER 11

"YOU WILL BE CAPTURED."

IN MID-APRIL, DURING EASTER WEEK, SHE CAME near the town of Melun. For ten years this town had been held by the English, and only six months before had been ceded to the Duke of Burgundy. The arrival of Joan and her troops stirred the townspeople to revolt. The uprising from within and the siege from without caused the Burgundians to surrender, and the town was taken.

At Melun, as Joan stood before the ramparts, the voices of Saint Catherine and Saint Margaret came to her again. They spoke no advice, only a warning. "Daughter of God," they said, "you will be captured before St. John's Day." It was bitter news for Joan, but not unexpected. "Then let me die quickly without suffering long captivity," she pleaded. "Do not be frightened," the voices said. "Resign yourself. God will help you."

The voices came to her every day after that to comfort and reassure her. St. John's Day was June 24, little more than two months hence, but Joan felt she must continue her striving until the last. From Melun she went north to Lagny, a town east of Paris on the river Marne. Lagny was loyal to King Charles, but it was being terrorized by a band of freebooters who were roaming the countryside. The French struck, and the marauders were vanquished. Their leader, a Burgundian captain named Franquet d'Arras, was captured, tried, and executed.

Although the reprisal against d'Arras was carried out fairly, the Burgundians later accused Joan of violating the laws of feudal warfare and of being needlessly cruel. D'Arras' execution was held against her later by her enemies, as was another incident that took place at Lagny. A baby had died there before it could be baptized, and the townspeople sent for Joan. Together with a number of maidens in the town, she knelt in the church before an image of the Virgin and prayed. According to Joan, the child's lifeless body was "as black as my tunic," but when the prayers were over, the baby yawned three times and his color returned. Quickly the infant was baptized; then he died once more, his soul now safe.

To Joan's friends and supporters that incident helped prove that she was a saint. To her enemies and detractors it was further evidence that she was a witch—and they would use every bit of evidence they had against her.

The truce between Duke Philip and King Charles finally expired on April 17 after many delays and extensions. Almost at once Duke Philip and a great army set out for Compiègne, a key city that lay on the Oise River and was considered the gateway to the north.

Compiègne had sworn fealty to King Charles shortly before the attack on Paris. At that time La Tremoïlle had been made governor, but the citizens of Compiègne rejected him and clamored for their own garrison commander, a knight named Guillaume de Flavy. Flavy was a hot-tempered man whose sense of duty was so great that he would gladly defend the city to the death.

Duke Philip took several French strongholds along the way, and by mid-May he was bivouacked before the town of Choisy, between Soissons and Compiègne. Joan, who had left Lagny early in May, arrived in Compiègne with her army, her knights, and the King's representative, Regnault of Chartres. A council of war was held. With the enemy so close at hand, and with the possibility of Compiègne being taken, the French decided to attack.

Joan and the army rode to Soissons, hoping to begin the assault there and surprise the Burgundians from the rear. But the commander of the city refused to open the gates to them. Instead of going forward to commence an attack, the army broke up, and Joan and a handful of men returned to Compiègne, disappointed.

About a week later, late in the afternoon of May 23, Joan rode out of Compiègne again. The Italian knight Bartolomeo Baretta and his company were behind her, as were archers, crossbowmen, and men-at-arms. Joan had little to do with the planning of this assault on the Burgundians, for as she said later, "From the time it was revealed to me at Melun that I would be captured, I left the military matters as much as possible to the captains of war."

Outside the city, the Burgundians had taken up positions in several villages along the far bank of the Oise. Jean de Luxembourg, Philip's second-in-command, was encamped some two miles upriver from Compiègne at Clairoix. Duke Philip, with his main force, was also in the region. Burgundian troops held the village of Margny, on a hill across the river from Compiègne, and five hundred English soldiers were stationed at Venette a few miles southwest. Clearly, Duke Philip was preparing a move in strength.

Taking the offensive, the French knights crossed the bridge from Compiègne. They rode over the low-lying meadow beyond the river leading to the high ground where Margny stood. To cover the cavalry, Captain Flavy had posted gunners and archers near the bridgehead. And he ordered small boats placed on the river so that, if necessary, the men could cross back to shelter in a hurry. These tactical steps were wise and well executed, but the French had a powerful human factor working against them. Jean de Luxembourg was in Margny that day to discuss the planned attack on Compiègne. When Flavy's horsemen galloped up the hill to begin their attack, Luxembourg sent a swift messenger to Clairoix to summon reinforcements. Then he joined in the defense of Margny.

Now the French force, with Joan in the lead, burst into the Burgundian camp. The fighting was fierce enough, but Joan's men seemed to lack the spirit they once had. They were pushed out of the village. They rallied, but Luxembourg's reinforcements, hard-riding knights of England and Burgundy, began to arrive. A cry was sounded among Joan's frightened men: "Every man for himself! Back to the city!" They turned and rushed down the hill, and many of them dashed wildly through the meadow. They pushed aboard the waiting boats and jammed the bridgehead. Nearly four hundred of them were killed in the battle or in the subsequent rout, while the Burgundians suffered no losses and only a few wounded.

Flavy and his gunners and archers were supposed to be covering the main French force. Possibly he could not order them to fire on the enemy for fear of hitting retreating Frenchmen.

However, he should have come out of the city with his garrison to cut off the English as they raced up from Venette. And he should have gone to Joan's aid when she stubbornly refused to turn back. Instead, seeing the Burgundians and the English nearing the bridgehead, he had the drawbridge raised and the city gates closed. The enemy was locked out now, but so was Joan.

Some chroniclers are certain that Flavy's was an act of treachery, for he was the nephew of Archbishop Regnault—and thus possibly involved in the plot to discredit Joan. Surely he was a ruthless man. He was capable of murder, and if it had suited his ends to rescue Joan, he probably would have done so. But, in any case, he did not.

Joan, cut off and surrounded, was fighting her way toward the bridgehead. Only a few Frenchmen were left with her, but they were outnumbered by their opponents and were finally overwhelmed. An enemy archer caught hold of Joan's cloak and dragged her from her horse, demanding that she make submission. "I have already made submission and plighted my faith to another," she replied, "and to Him will I keep my word."

Another archer approached her, declaring himself of noble birth. It was to him she finally surrendered. She was bound fast and carried off to Margny. St. John's Day was a month away, but Joan was already a captive.

CHAPTER 12

PRISON

IT WAS CUSTOMARY IN WAR TO HOLD A CAPTURED chief or nobleman for ransom. But the case of Joan's capture was not an ordinary one. Too much was at stake. In effect, the Maid had torn up the Treaty of Troyes. Because of her, the Dauphin had been anointed king of France; and under her leadership, the French, until recently, had shown that they were a match for the English and the Burgundians. In addition, Joan had claimed that divine inspiration had brought about these achievements, without the aid of any churchmen. Thus it is not surprising that after Joan's capture one of the first voices raised in satisfaction was Archbishop Regnault's. In a letter to his diocese of Reims he wrote that Joan had deserved capture "because she would not take advice, but would follow her own will." He was stating, in effect, that she deserved her hapless fate because she would not submit either to his authority or to that of the Church.

Similarly satisfied by the turn of events was La Tremoïlle, who, according to a chronicler, was "overcome with delight." But these men represented only a small, though powerful, minority. Most of France was grief-stricken at the news that Joan was in the hands of her enemies. Public prayers and special masses were said in many of the towns she had liberated. And letters were sent to King Charles, imploring him to pay whatever sum might be necessary to free the Maid.

But Charles did nothing. Perhaps he believed Joan was a prisoner because God had withdrawn His favor from her and that helping her would defy God's will. Yet, since the charges against Joan were aimed indirectly at Charles, it is difficult to appreciate his passivity.

Actually, Bedford and the enemies of France were anxious to do more than merely discredit the Maid and the King she had crowned. To justify their fear of her and their losses in combat—and to win the French people away from Charles VII— they could not treat her simply as a prisoner of war. They had to prove that Joan had not really been sent by God and then burn her as a witch and a heretic. To this end her trial was prepared. In Joan's case a verdict was established first, and justice was tailored to fit it.

Joan was yielded by her captors to the Burgundian Jean

de Luxembourg, who held her prisoner for five months. Although treated kindly, she made two attempts to escape. Once, at the castle of Beaulieu, she succeeded in getting as far as the gates before the porter caught her. Luxembourg then removed her to his castle at Beaurevoir, where the news reached her that she was to be turned over to the English. In desperation Joan leaped from the castle tower and fell to the ground below. She was knocked unconscious by the impact; otherwise she received no injuries—which seemed miraculous since she probably fell about seventy feet. She was recaptured, of course, and was later accused of having tried to commit suicide. Joan's enemies would stop at nothing; her every word, her every action, was distorted and used against her.

In November she was handed over to the English, and the sum of six thousand francs was paid to Luxembourg. Joan was moved from castle to castle, farther north and west, until finally she was conveyed to Rouen and imprisoned. Her cell was narrow and damp, and she was chained hand and foot to a log. Five surly men-at-arms guarded her.

She begged to be taken to an ecclesiastical prison, since she was to be tried by the Church, but her pleas went unheard. The English were taking no chances now that they had her. They turned her over to the Church for trial, but their intentions were stated clearly by the Duke of Bedford in a letter of transfer in which he said, "Nevertheless, it is our intention to retake and resecure the said Joan should it happen that she be not convicted as guilty . . ."

An ecclesiastical court was summoned in January 1431. The chief judge was Pierre Cauchon, Bishop of Beauvais and a bitter enemy of King Charles. He was actually a high councilor in the pay of the English crown, and he hoped by his management of Joan's trial to be awarded the rich archbishopric of Rouen, which was then vacant. Cauchon was prepared to mete out the kind of justice the English were thirsting for—the execution of a heretic—and he could do it only in Rouen. Another major city would have had an archbishop under whose jurisdiction Joan would have come. And though Cauchon also had to take orders, his direct superior was Archbishop Regnault, who had always opposed Joan.

There is some question whether Cauchon had the right to try Joan, for she may not have belonged under his jurisdiction after all. No proof was ever shown that she had committed her alleged crimes within the diocese of Beauvais. In addition, a controversy has raged for five hundred years over the legality of Joan's trial. In form, the proceedings may well have been legal, but few would argue that they were just. Nor was there any real basis for the trial. Joan had already been examined by a high Church tribunal at Poitiers and had been cleared of any suspicion of having come from the Devil. How could she be tried as a heretic when Archbishop Regnault himself had attested to her piety and honesty?

None of these questions disturbed Cauchon. He made plans for a full-dress trial. Instead of having six or eight judges, the usual number for a trial of heresy, he selected more than fifty high churchmen, and almost a hundred more were involved from time to time. Regnault of Chartres remained quietly on the sidelines, and King Charles secluded himself in his castles on the Loire.

Joan, meanwhile, was locked in her prison cell. She was visited by curious nobles, spied on from holes in the walls, and stared at like an animal by the coarse English guards. Indeed it seemed that Cauchon had made certain that only the basest sort of soldiers would be her jailers—men who continually hurled abuse at her and who kept her in constant fear of being assaulted.

CHAPTER 13

INTERROGATION

ON FEBRUARY 21, IN THE CHAPEL OF THE CASTLE of Rouen, the court held its first public session. In a room nearby, England's nine-year-old king, Henry VI, was at play. This was as close as Joan would ever come to meeting him— still only a child, but still her archenemy.

As the clerk was reading the letters and documents that empowered Cauchon to try his prisoner, Joan was brought in. She looked pale and haggard after her many weeks in chains, and she still wore male clothing. The sight of this astounded many monks who were present, for did not the Bible forbid women to wear men's clothes? Joan's appearance weighed against her from the start, and her refusal to dress differently helped, eventually, to convict her.

Cauchon opened the proceedings by stating that for the sake of Joan's conscience, and to hasten the trial, "she should answer the whole truth to the questions put to her on these matters of faith."

Joan said, "I do not know what you wish to examine me on. Perhaps you might ask me things I would not want to tell you." The Bishop asked, "Will you swear to speak the truth upon those things which you are asked concerning the faith, which you know?"

She replied that she would gladly swear to all that concerned her parents and what she had done since leaving Domrémy. But the nature of her revelations from God had never been told to anyone except King Charles, and she would tell them to no one else, not even to save her life. At last, however, she knelt and placed her hands on the Gospels. She swore to answer truthfully any questions on matters of faith with which she was familiar but insisted she would keep silent about her revelations.

Cauchon seemed satisfied with this, and the examination began. Joan was asked about her baptism, her childhood, and her family, and one judge wanted to know her age. (She said she thought she was nineteen.) Other routine questions followed, and finally Cauchon offered to trade Joan's chains for her promise not to try to escape. Joan replied that she had wished to escape before "and still wish to escape, as is lawful for any prisoner." And on this note of defiance the first session ended.

There were five more public sessions, which covered the Maid's entire career. The interrogation was exhausting, but Joan showed herself alert and capable in spite of her weariness. First one, then another of the canons and doctors questioned her, and she dealt firmly with each of them. Over and over they asked her to tell the truth about everything. And always she replied that there were things she had sworn never to disclose to anyone. "Would you have me perjure myself?" she asked. Many times, when the questions were impertinent, or when they seemed foolish, she replied, "Pass on." She said "Pass on" when asked if she thought it well to have attacked Paris on a feast day. She knew military commanders were not expected to observe such days in the middle of campaigns.

One of the judges suddenly asked her, "Do you know whether you are in God's grace?" Another monk put in, "That is a ponderous question. She need not answer it."

Indeed it was a ponderous question, and hardly a fair one either. As a good Christian she could not know for certain and could not truthfully answer Yes. But if she answered No, she would have placed herself outside the pale. Deftly she replied, "If I am not in God's grace, I pray God to put me there; if I am, may God keep me there."

By asking that question, the court had hoped to trick her. They made other attempts too, inquiring about her saints. Did they have hair? (Her answer: "It is a comfort to know that they have.") Was Saint Michael naked? ("Do you think God has nothing with which to clothe him?") Did Saint Margaret speak in English? ("Why should she speak in English when she is not on the English side?")

To a particularly pointed question about her prophecies, Joan replied, "Before seven years are past the English will lose a greater stake than they did at Orléans, for they will lose everything in France." In answer to repeated queries about the secret she shared with Charles, she merely said, "For three weeks at Chinon and Poitiers I was examined by churchmen. Send to Poitiers and ask for their records." Each time she said this, the line of questioning was changed. The fact that she had been examined and cleared by the tribunal at Poitiers was embarrassing to the court.

On March 3, the last day of the public sessions, Joan was asked, "Do those of your party firmly believe you were sent from God?" And she replied, "I do not know whether they do, and you ought to ask them for their opinion. But whether they do or not, nevertheless I am sent from God."

The fine, full-dress trial had been a failure. Nothing whatever—of heresy, witchcraft, or sorcery—had been proved against her. Actually, she had shown herself to good advantage.

Her answers, calm and direct, had impressed many of her judges. One of Cauchon's supporters, Jean Lohier, a doctor of both Church and civil law, stated firmly that the trial was null and void.

It was being held, said Lohier, in a place where the judges did not feel free to express their true opinions. He pointed out that the trial concerned the honor of King Charles but no one there represented him. In addition, there were no documents to support the accusations, and the accused had no lawyer. Lohier was later reported to have said to a notary, "You can see for yourself how they are proceeding. They will try to convict her by her exact words. If, for instance, in speaking of her visions, she were to say, 'It seems to me,' instead of 'I know for certain,' it is my opinion that not a single man would have the effrontery to condemn her."

Ignoring the rumbles of doubt and opposition, Cauchon announced: "The trial continues without interruption." Then with a small circle of carefully chosen supporters, he quickly prepared the evidence and formulated the accusations. The trial would be continued in private; Cauchon had no intention of bringing this case before the public again until he had his indictments ready.

For the next seven days the cross-examination was conducted in Joan's prison cell. Instead of fifty masters and doctors, there was only Cauchon and his deputy, two or three doctors of theology, and two notaries to keep the record. Again and again Joan was asked about her voices and her revelations to King Charles. But she held fast to her contention that everything she had done was at God's command. Although she was worn out—it was Lent and she was fasting and also recovering from a debilitating illness—she maintained her defiance.

The question of her clothing was continually raised. Once she was told she would be allowed to hear mass, which she had not been permitted to do, if she would change into feminine garb. She said she would do so if she could put on her male clothing after the service. From the beginning of her career, she had insisted on being treated as a warrior among fellow warriors. She had no intention of risking the perils of being regarded as a defenseless woman—certainly not now when she was an unarmed prisoner. When she was urged to change clothing without any conditions, she said, "Make me a long woman's dress and I shall hear mass in it, but I beg you to allow me to hear mass without changing."

On March 18 the private investigation was ended. It was Passion Sunday, but Joan was not allowed to hear mass, for she still refused to change her attire. Little more than a week later, on March 27, her trial was resumed again in public. A list of seventy charges had been drawn up against her. It had been decided that these would be read to her, and according to the records of the trial, "if Joan refused to answer [the charges], after she had been canonically admonished, they should be held to be confessed."

Joan was now offered a defense lawyer to be chosen from among the judges who had been summoned into court, and who were Cauchon's own men. To this she replied, "For the counsel you offer me, I thank you, but I have no intention of departing from the counsel of Our Lord."

The seventy charges took two days to read. They were a recapitulation of the rumors, misstatements, and false tales about her that had been covered during the preceding weeks. "The said accused . . . has performed, composed, and commanded many charms and superstitions; she has been deified and has permitted herself to be adored and venerated; she has called up demons and evil spirits, has consulted and frequented them . . ."

Joan vehemently repudiated the charges. She insisted she had not blasphemed God. She repeated that she was a good Christian, that "it is for God to make revelations to whom He pleases," and that she referred herself to the judgment of God. By thus denying the authority of Cauchon's court, she was unknowingly aiding his case against her. For now the Bishop could claim that she was elevating herself above the authority of the Church. That was his only substantial charge against her; he knew he could not find a single witness to verify his other charges. Joan was returned to prison, and the seventy articles were condensed to twelve.

These twelve articles contained gross distortions and twistings of her words, false charges, and half-truths. The articles were sent to a number of clerical authorities for immediate ratification. Joan, who was not permitted to review the twelve articles, had grown ill again. The strain of the questioning, and of her sleeplessness and ill-treatment, made it impossible for her to recover fully. This time she became so sick that the English feared she might die a natural death and slip from their grasp.

But she did not die. She spent much of the next month convalescing, chained to her cot. During that time Cauchon and other members of the clergy visited her often to urge that she submit to the Church's authority and confess all her sins. Earlier in her trial Joan had offered to go before the Pope in person; now again she offered to submit to papal judgment. But few of her judges favored this. It was vitally important for the political purposes of Cauchon's English superiors that Joan be summarily condemned by the court at Rouen and be made to confess her crimes.

CHAPTER 14

TORTURE AND TRICKERY

ON MAY 9 SHE WAS LED INTO A TORTURE CHAMBER, and Cauchon warned her, "If you do not tell the truth, you shall be tortured so that you can be brought back to the path of truth for the salvation of your soul and your body, which you expose to great dangers by your lying tricks."

Joan looked around the ugly room—at the rack, the glowing braziers, the knives and spikes, hooks and pincers. And then she replied, "Should you tear my limbs from me and drive my soul from my body, I could tell you nothing else; and if I did say anything, I would always say afterward that you had dragged it from me by force." Cauchon was growing angry now, and impatient. Much as he may have desired it, he knew that torturing Joan would avail him nothing. So did most of the religious scholars consulted in the matter. Their feelings were summarized best by a cleric who insisted that torture "might spoil the effect of such an admirably conducted trial."

So the Maid was returned to her cell. It was difficult to know what to do with anyone as stubborn as she except to try to wear her down slowly and keep before her the clear threat of a painful death by fire. For in the eyes of her judges, her saints were demons, and everything she had accomplished was the result of sorcery and witchcraft.

On May 23, 1431, exactly one year after her capture outside Compiègne, Joan the Maid heard the Church's indictment against her. She was led from her cell to a room in the castle where Cauchon and ten other Church dignitaries had gathered. A doctor of theology, Pierre Maurice, read the indictment and then preached a lengthy and kindly sermon. In it he warned that according to many religious authorities, Joan's visions were false and superstitious, and he implored her to recant. "I admonish and beg you," Maurice said, "by the pity you have for the passion of your Creator, by the love you bear for the salvation of your body and soul, to correct these errors and return to the ways of truth by obedience to the Church and submission to her judgment and decision."

It seemed that the entire force of the Church—indeed, of all contemporary theology—was being hurled against her. However, despite the months of illness and the ceaseless torture of her spirit, Joan remained defiant. "If at this moment I saw the stake, the fagots, the executioner lighting the fire, and if I stood in the middle of it, I would not say anything else, and I would say until death only what I said at the trial."

On May 24, Joan was taken to the cemetery behind the Church of St. Ouen, outside the castle walls. Two wooden platforms had been built. Cauchon and most of the judges sat on the larger one; Joan was placed on the smaller one along with a notary, a bailiff, and a doctor of theology, Guillaume Erard. A host of soldiers and priests and half the city of Rouen turned out to witness the spectacle, and the crowd seethed with anticipation.

Guillaume Erard rose to his feet and began his sermon; a long oration in which he spoke of Joan as a heretic, a monster, and a witch—and condemned Charles for having been influenced by her. To drive home his thesis, he suddenly pointed to Joan and cried, "Your King is a heretic!" Joan interrupted the cleric, "With all due respect to you," she began, "I swear that my King is the most noble Christian of all Christians."

An usher silenced her, and Erard continued. When he had finished his sermon he asked Joan if she would agree that all her deeds and sayings, which had been condemned, were vile. She said, "I refer myself to God and to our Holy Father the Pope."

Cauchon replied, "The Pope is too far away. All of us are competent to be judges." Three times she was urged to recant.

Then Cauchon began reading the sentence that would turn her over to the civil authorities to be burned at the stake.

The priests began clamoring to Joan to do as she was advised—to put on women's dress, submit to the Church, and save herself from death. The noise was deafening. Joan looked around. She saw the executioner waiting with his cart and the shouting crowd pressing closer around her. It must have been an awful moment for her, ill and weary of her prison life and the strain of debating for so long with these mighty clerics. Perhaps in her imagination she could already feel the hideous pain of the fire.

Suddenly she cried, "I submit to the judgment of the Church." She then renounced her visions and revelations, and said several times that she no longer believed in her voices. She had recanted! This caused excitement in the crowd and an angry outburst from the English soldiers. It looked as if Joan would escape after all.

The Form of Recantation was read to her—only seven or eight lines—which contained the declarations that she had sinned, that she had broken the laws of God and the Church, and that she would henceforth be obedient to the Church, would no longer bear arms, dress as a man, or wear her hair short. She repeated these words and signed the document by making a cross. There is some basis for suspecting that what she signed was not the same form as the one which had been read to her. One chronicler insists that a substitution was made and that the paper Joan signed contained the confession that her revelations and her voices were false. But Joan could not read and knew nothing of what she had signed. She was happy, though, and it was said that she smiled; now, she thought, she would be out of the grasp of the hated English.

In spite of the howls of protest from the soldiers, who had been throwing stones and brandishing their swords, Cauchon then had a milder sentence read. This one condemned Joan to life imprisonment instead of death. Jubilantly, Joan said, "Now you churchmen, take me to your prison. Let me be no longer in the hands of the English." For this is what the clamoring priests had promised her. She had agreed to put on women's clothes, for she expected to have female guardians around her—and to be treated more like a penitent than a prisoner.

However, by the terms of the bargain that Cauchon had made with Bedford, Joan was to be retaken and resecured by the English, since she had not been convicted. Even though she had recanted and signed what the priests had given her, she was not sent to a Church prison. Instead, Cauchon ordered, "Take her back to the place you brought her from," and she was returned to her dark cell in the castle tower. Her head was shaved and she was dressed in a long gown.

Cauchon's trickery had been effective. The Church had

been appeased, for Joan had confessed her sins and renounced her visions. And soon she would fall into a trap that would lead to her death; this certainly would please the English. Cauchon had arranged it all very skillfully.

Although Joan was forbidden now to wear masculine attire—for she had agreed she would not—her old clothes were not taken away from her. According to one account they were placed in a bag that was left in the prison, perhaps in a corner of her cell. She was guarded not by priests or nuns, but by the same vile soldiery that had jeered at her and tried to harm her throughout her previous imprisonment. During the next three days, even more abuse was heaped on her; some reports indicate that she may have been beaten. Then, in a final act of treachery, her female attire was stolen while she slept. She had no choice but to put on her old clothes again—and thus break her oath.

Hearing of Joan's relapse, Cauchon and other Church officials visited her prison cell on May 28, 1431. They found her in tears, her face dull with misery. She was wearing a tunic, long hose, and a jerkin with the hood pulled over her shaven head. As the merciless judges cross-examined her once more, she cried out, "My voices have told me . . . that I did very wrong in [recanting] and that I must confess that I did wrong. It was fear of the fire that made me say that which I said . . ."

She must have realized finally that the English would never

let her go, that they intended to dishonor her name and destroy her, one way or another. In reality Joan had signed her own death warrant by putting on male clothing again, and she made no further effort to save herself. As the Bishop came out of the prison tower he met an English nobleman in the courtyard and said to him significantly, "Farewell. Be of good cheer, she is ours now."

CHAPTER 15

SENTENCED TO THE STAKE

ON WEDNESDAY MORNING, MAY 30, THE MAID left her cell for the last time. Beside her was the young friar who had heard her last confession and had given her communion. She was placed in a cart, and with a guard of eighty men-at-arms taken to the old market square of Rouen. All along the way crowds came out to stare at the pitiable girl who had terrified the armies of England and had led France to so many unexpected victories.

She was placed on a platform opposite a large dais on which her judges sat. There she stood for nearly an hour while a lengthy sermon was read. When it was ended, Joan's final sentence was pronounced by Bishop Cauchon. By its terms, Joan was given over to secular authorities to be burned, for the Church could not carry out any civil punishments. Joan burst into a passion of weeping. Death by fire is a cruel torment. She began to pray aloud in a trembling, pitiful voice, and many of those who watched wept with her. The high churchmen who had condemned her wept too, and some of them were so overcome they had to leave the market place.

She turned to the crowd and implored all those who stood there "to forgive the harm I have done you as I forgive the harm you have done me." And to several priests whom she saw with tears in their eyes, she said, "All you priests who are here, I beg you to say a mass for me, every one of you."

After half an hour of praying, Joan asked for a crucifix; and it was an English soldier, moved by the sight of her, who fashioned a cross by tying two pieces of wood together. She took the cross, kissed it, and pressed it to her breast. Then she saw two priests standing near her. To one of them she called, "I beg of you, go into that church there and bring the crucifix. Hold it just before my eyes until I die." The priest brought it to her and held it up for her to kiss. Now the English soldiers roared their impatience, and the bailiff shouted an order to the executioner, "Take her to the stake."

She was rudely hauled to the foot of the stake, which had been set on a high scaffold made of plaster. On her head a paper cap was placed bearing the words Heretic, Relapsed, Apostate, Idolatress. She stepped on the fagots that had been heaped about the scaffold, and the two priests followed her.

She kissed the crucifix once again, and then the executioner bound her to the stake. She called upon Saint Michael, and the executioner set fire to the fagots.

The two priests were still at her side. She pleaded with them to get down—but to hold the crucifix up in front of her so she could continue to see it. Quickly the flames rose about her feet. Yet above the snapping of the fire, Joan's voice could still be heard calling on God, the Archangel, and her saints. Some witnesses thought they heard her begging for holy water.

Suddenly she shrieked, "Jesus, Jesus, Jesus!" The fire enveloped her. Once more, half-stifled by her anguish, her voice cried out, "Jesus!"

Nothing more was heard from her. Her saints had promised her freedom and martyrdom. Now she had gained both.

CHAPTER 16

THE LEGEND OF JOAN

THE MAID WAS DEAD. HER ASHES HAD BEEN gathered up and thrown into the Seine's filthy waters. Now the English royal council sent out letters to princes and churchmen everywhere proclaiming that a powerful and dangerous heretic had been destroyed. But what Joan had achieved could not be stamped out; nor could her memory be eliminated as easily as her body had been burned.

She had warned her judges that within seven years the English would lose everything in France. She had foreseen what was inevitable, for she herself had been responsible for it.

Soon after Joan's death, the regent of England made plans to have young Henry VI crowned king at Reims. But it soon became obvious that this was impossible. The people of Reims, who had held out so long against England's threats, and who had remained staunchly loyal to Charles VII, would not permit it. The English then decided to crown the youngster in Paris, and they took elaborate pains to smuggle him into the city. In December 1431, six months after Joan's execution, Henry VI of England was crowned king of France. But his coronation was a hopeless gesture; in the eyes of France, Charles VII remained the anointed king.

Although French and English forces continued to skirmish, King Charles and his councilors worked in earnest to secure peace. The tension that had existed for years between France and Burgundy was eased somewhat by the death of Bedford in 1435. After all, the agreements between England and the Duke of Burgundy had been made with Bedford, not the English crown. With Bedford out of the way, an accord could be reached between the Burgundians and the French. A treaty was finally signed in September 1435. By its terms the Duke of Burgundy was recognized as an independent lord, and he was granted possession of much of the land that had been so long in dispute.

Early in 1436 Paris opened its gates at last to King Charles of France. The city's English garrison, starved into submission, was allowed to march out of the city and sail down the Seine to Rouen. The English continued to be pushed gradually out of France until, by April 1450, only small parts of Normandy and Guienne were still under England's control.

The French closed in. They now had a weapon more deadly than the dreaded English longbow: artillery. A new light cannon had been developed by the French for use against enemy troops. Its leaden bullets tore huge gaps in the English lines, dropping archers and knights alike, no matter how heavily armored they were.

By the end of 1450 all of Normandy was French once more, and three years later the last battle in Guienne was fought. England's Lord Talbot, who had been captured by Joan and her "fair Duke" Alençon at Patay, marched with his troops to meet a French force standing before the town of Castillon. Talbot ordered a direct assault, which was stopped by French cannons. Struck by a bullet, Talbot fell dead in a trench before the city, and his army was destroyed.

Joan's third task had now been achieved, although she herself had been dead for twenty-two years. The English had been driven out of France.

In 1455 she received another trial, this time in Paris—which now belonged to the French crown—and with loyal Frenchmen sitting in judgment. Joan's mother and brothers had brought the formal action. Historians describe the moving scene that took place at Notre Dame in Paris on the November day when the aged widow, her tears masked by a veil of mourning, presented her claim that Joan had been unjustly punished. The judges agreed to reopen the case.

In pleading that Joan's reputation be cleared, the d'Arc family was acting on the counsel of King Charles' advisers. He remained outside the proceedings, however, for the sake of relations between England and France and the Church. Bringing about the investigation was a small gift indeed from the King to the girl who had given him his crown. He had not felt an obligation to defend her before; now that his land was free and he felt secure, he tried to make amends for his former inaction.

At the new trial, called the Rehabilitation, testimony was given by Joan's childhood friends, and by priests, squires, townsfolk, peasants, and knights. Her personal squire, d'Aulon, was there, now a rich and respected knight. So were Alençon, Dunois, and her chaplain, Pasquerel, tottering with age.

Many of the clerics who had been responsible for the Maid's death were called to the Rehabilitation trial to present their evidence. Some could remember nothing, but many gave testimony that helped prove Joan had been falsely condemned. Finally, on July 7, 1456, after the results of this trial had been submitted to the Pope, a new judgment was handed down. The sentence that had been pronounced in Rouen was annulled and declared invalid. Joan was innocent.

The Rehabilitation answered many of the questions that had puzzled people about Joan. Yet two significant questions remained unanswered—then as well as now. Who was she? What was she? For the past five centuries historians and theologians have searched vainly for answers.

It has been said, for example, that Joan's was a typical case of hysteria and that her visions were brought on by a neurosis, even insanity. It has also been argued that she was a true mystic; indeed, she was beatified by the Catholic Church in 1909 and finally admitted to the catalogue of saints in 1920.

Some scholars have insisted that Joan was but a tool of certain clerics, others that she was the tool of certain anticlerical noblemen. Still others have demeaned her as a simpleton who became a kind of good-luck symbol. And there are even a few scholars who say that she was the queen of a secret cult of witches whose ritual prescribed that she be burned to death, her ashes scattered abroad.

Her life has attracted poets, playwrights, essayists, and novelists—including such men as Shakespeare, Shaw, Voltaire, and Mark Twain. She has provided thousands of artists with the inspiration for paintings and sculptures, though not one authentic portrait was done in her lifetime.

Joan may have been any of the things her supporters and detractors have said—or none of them. The many facts that are known of her visions, her predictions, and her acts come from the records of her trial, the Rehabilitation, and the writings of her contemporaries. Studied carefully, these accounts provide a detailed report of the events of her life, but only a sketch of her character. Yet some conclusions about her can be drawn.

By her faith in herself and her absolute conviction in her purpose, she was able to give men the heart and strength to fight. She knew nothing of battle tactics or the rules of war. She proved to France that the English forces could be defeated; and they were. It is not necessary to know for certain whether she personally led her troops into the bloodiest part of the battle or whether, like her white standard, she was merely there as an inspiring symbol.

Nor can anyone ever know the truth about Joan's voices, her prophecies, or the miracles she was said to have performed. The devout may believe that her achievements were brought about by God; the skeptical may try to explain her deeds in terms of earthly phenomena. Only one thing is certain: Joan was an extraordinary person, possibly a genius.

Her answers at her trial and her behavior before her judges are proof enough of that. She was young, innocent, unlettered, alone and abandoned by her friends, surrounded by enemies. Yet she faced a continuous cross-examination by learned and powerful men of the Church, and she answered their questions with dignity, wry humor, and intelligence. She was no simpleton, no unsuspecting tool in someone else's hands. Did not Archbishop Regnault himself insist that "she would not take advice, but would follow her own will"?

Indeed, she was strong-willed, for she never ceased trying to achieve her purpose, even though to do so she had to drag along with her the whole of France, from the commonest soldier to the King himself.

Many historians have described Joan as a genius. But one man, Pierre Champion, analyzed her legend differently. He wrote of Joan: "She is entirely human—and never was humanity greater." This is perhaps the truest of the epitaphs that have been written of her.

Index

ABOUT THE AUTHOR

JAY WILLIAMS was born in Buffalo, New York and was edu-
cated at the University of Pennsylvania, Columbia University,
and the Art Students League. In addition to writing, Williams
worked as a vaudeville comedian and a Hollywood press
agent. During World War II he was awarded the Purple Heart
while serving with the 65th Infantry Division of the United
States Army. It was while serving in the war that Williams
published his first book, *The Stolen Oracle*.

Williams is perhaps best known for his popular children's
science fiction series, Danny Dunn, which he co-authored and
which continued from 1956 until 1977.

Williams was the author of over 75 picture books, children's
novels, adult mysteries and historical novels. He was the edi-
tor of several anthologies including the *Oxford Book of Modern
Fairy Tales*.

BOOKS IN THIS SERIES

✷STERLING POINT BOOKS